Articulating Reasons

Articulating Reasons

AN INTRODUCTION
TO INFERENTIALISM

◆ ◆ ◆

Robert B. Brandom

Harvard University Press
Cambridge, Massachusetts
London, England

First Harvard University Press paperback edition, 2001

Library of Congress Cataloging-in-Publication Data

Brandom, Robert.
  Articulating reasons : an introduction to inferentialism / Robert B. Brandom.
    p.   cm.
  Includes bibliographical references and index.
  ISBN 0-674-00158-3 (cloth)
  ISBN 0-674-00692-5 (pbk.)
    1. Language and languages—Philosophy. 2. Semantics (Philosophy)
3. Inference. 4. Reasoning. 5. Language and logic. 6. Expression
(Philosophy) I. Title.

P106.B6938 2000
121'.68—dc21   99-057756

*To my wife, Barbara, whose loving support
and patient indulgence over the years
mean more to me than I can say*

Acknowledgments

◆ ◆ ◆

The lectures on which this book is based evolved under the influence of the responses of many audiences to which different versions have been presented in recent years. Here and there it has been possible to acknowledge particular contributions, but the cumulative effect of all those smart people thinking these things through with me—and the debt I owe for it—is incalculable. I am profoundly grateful.

Contents

◆　◆　◆

Introduction

◆ ◆ ◆

I. Strategic Context: The Nature of the Conceptual

This is a book about the use and content of *concepts*. Its animating thought is that the meanings of linguistic expressions and the contents of intentional states, indeed, awareness itself, should be understood, to begin with, in terms of playing a distinctive kind of role in *reasoning*. The idea of privileging *inference* over *reference* in the order of semantic explanation is introduced and motivated in the first chapter. Subsequent chapters develop that approach by using it to address a variety of philosophically important issues and problems: practical reasoning and the role of normative concepts in the theory of action, perception and the role of assessments of reliability in epistemology, the expressive role distinctive of singular terms and predicates (which, as subsentential expressions, cannot play the directly inferential role of premise or conclusion), propositional attitude ascriptions and the representational dimension of concept use, and the nature of conceptual objectivity. Although the discussion is intended to be intelligible in its own right—in each individual chapter, as well as collectively—it may nonetheless be helpful to step back a bit from the project pursued here and to situate it in the larger context of theoretical issues, possibilities, and approaches within which it takes shape.

The overall topic is the nature of the conceptual as such. This choice already entails certain significant emphases of attention: within the philosophy of mind, on awareness in the sense of *sapience* rather than of mere sentience; within semantics, on specifically *conceptual* content, to the detriment of concern with other sorts of contentfulness; within pragmatics, on singling out *discursive* (that is, concept-using) practice from the background of various other kinds of skillful doing. The aim is to focus on the conceptual in order to elaborate a relatively clear notion of the kind of *awareness* of something that consists in applying a concept to it—paradigmatically by saying or thinking something about it.

Addressing this topic requires making a series of choices of fundamental explanatory strategy. The resulting commitments need to be brought out into the open because they shape any approach to the conceptual in such important ways. Making this background of orienting commitments explicit serves to place a view in a philosophical space of alternatives. Features of an account that otherwise express nearly invisible (because only implicit) assumptions then show up as calling for decisions, which are subject to determinate sorts of challenges and demands for justification. The major axes articulating the region inhabited by the line of thought pursued here can be presented as a series of stark binary oppositions, which collectively make it possible to map the surrounding terrain.

1. *Assimilation* or *Differentiation* of the Conceptual?

One fork in the methodological road concerns the relative priority accorded to the *continuities* and *dis*continuities between discursive and nondiscursive creatures: the similarities and differences between the judgments and actions of concept users, on the one hand, and the uptake of environmental information and instrumental interventions of non–concept-using organisms and artifacts, on the other. We can ask how sharp this distinction is—that is, to what extent and in what ways the possibility of intermediate cases can be made intelligible. And more or less independently of the answer to this question, it is possible for theorists to differ as to whether they *start* by describing a common genus and go on to elaborate differentiae (whether qualitative or in terms of some quantitative ordering by a particular kind of complexity), as opposed to beginning with an account of what is distinctive of the conceptual, which is only later placed in a larger frame encompassing the doings of less capable systems. Of course, wherever the story starts, it will need to account both for the ways in which concept use is like the comportments of nondiscursive creatures and the ways in which it differs. Theories that *assimilate* conceptually structured activity to the nonconceptual activity out of which it arises (in evolutionary, historical, and individual-developmental terms) are in danger of failing to make enough of the difference. Theories that adopt the converse strategy, addressing themselves at the outset to what is *distinctive* of or exceptional about the conceptual, court the danger of not doing justice to generic similarities. The difference in emphasis and order of explanation can express substantive theoretical commitments.

Along this dimension, the story told here falls into the second class: *dis*continuities between the conceptual and non- or preconceptual are to the fore. The discussion is motivated by a concern with what is special about or characteristic of the conceptual as such. I am more interested in what separates concept users from non–concept users than in what unites them. This distinguishes my project from that of many in contemporary semantic theory (for instance, Dretske, Fodor, and Millikan), as well as from the classical American pragmatists, and perhaps from the later Wittgenstein as well.

2. Conceptual *Platonism* or *Pragmatism?*

Here is another strategic methodological issue. An account of the conceptual might explain the *use* of concepts in terms of a prior understanding of conceptual *content*. Or it might pursue a complementary explanatory strategy, beginning with a story about the practice or activity of applying concepts, and elaborating on that basis an understanding of conceptual content. The first can be called a *platonist* strategy, and the second a *pragmatist* (in this usage, a species of functionalist) strategy. One variety of semantic or conceptual platonism in this sense would identify the content typically expressed by declarative sentences and possessed by beliefs with sets of possible worlds, or with truth conditions otherwise specified. At some point it must then explain how associating such content with sentences and beliefs contributes to our understanding of how it is proper to use sentences in making claims, and to deploy beliefs in reasoning and guiding action. The pragmatist direction of explanation, by contrast, seeks to explain how the use of linguistic expressions, or the functional role of intentional states, confers conceptual content on them.

The view expounded in these pages is a kind of conceptual pragmatism (broadly, a form of functionalism) in this sense. It offers an account of knowing (or believing, or saying) *that* such and such is the case in terms of knowing *how* (being able) to *do* something. It approaches the contents of conceptually *explicit* propositions or principles from the direction of what is *implicit* in practices of using expressions and acquiring and deploying beliefs. 'Assertion', 'claim', 'judgment', and 'belief' are all systematically ambiguous expressions—and not merely by coincidence. The sort of pragmatism adopted here seeks to explain what is assert*ed* by appeal to features of assert*ings,* what is claim*ed* in terms of claim*ings,* what is judg*ed* by judg*ings,* and what is believ*ed* by the role of believ*ings* (indeed, what is expressed by expressings of it)—in general, the content by the act, rather than the other way around.

3. Is *Mind* or *Language* the Fundamental Locus of Intentionality?

Concepts are applied in the realm of *language* by the public use of sentences and other linguistic expressions. They are applied in the realm of *mind* by the private adoption of and rational reliance on beliefs and other intentional states. The philosophical tradition from Descartes to Kant took for granted a *mentalistic* order of explanation that privileged the mind as the native and original locus of concept use, relegating language to a secondary, late-coming, merely instrumental role in communicating to others thoughts already full-formed in a prior mental arena within the individual. The period since then has been characterized by a growing appreciation of the significance of language for thought and mindedness generally, and a questioning of the picture of language as a more or less convenient tool for expressing thoughts intelligible as contentful apart from any consideration of the possibility of *saying* what one is *thinking*. The twentieth century has been the century of language in philosophical thought, accelerating into something like a reversal of the traditional order of explanation. Thus Dummett defends a *linguistic* theory of intentionality: "We have opposed throughout the view of assertion as the expression of an interior act of judgment; judgment, rather, is the interiorization of the external act of assertion."[1] Dummett's claim is emblematic of views (put forward in different forms by thinkers such as Sellars and Geach) that see language use as antecedently and independently intelligible, and so as available to provide a model on the basis of which one could then come to understand mental acts and occurrences analogically: taking thinking as a kind of inner saying. Such a view just turns the classical early modern approach on its head.

Davidson claims that to be a believer one must be an interpreter of the speech of others, but that "neither language nor thinking can be fully explained in terms of the other, and neither has conceptual priority. The two are, indeed, linked in the sense that each requires the other in order to be understood, but the linkage is not so complete that either suffices, even when reasonably reinforced, to explicate the other."[2] Although Davidson shares some important motivations with Dummett's purely linguistic theory, in fact these two views illustrate an important difference between two ways in which one might give prominence to linguistic practice in thinking about the use of concepts. Davidson's claim, by contrast to Dummett's, serves to epitomize a *relational* view of the significance of language for sapience: taking it that concept use is not intelligible in a context that does not include language use, but not insisting that linguistic practices can be made sense of without appeal at the same time to intentional states such as belief.

The line of thought pursued here is in this sense a *relational linguistic* approach to the conceptual. Concept use is treated as an essentially linguistic affair. Claiming and believing are two sides of one coin—not in the sense that every belief must be asserted nor that every assertion must express a belief, but in the sense that neither the activity of believing nor that of asserting can be made sense of independently of the other, and that their conceptual contents are essentially, and not just accidentally, capable of being the contents indifferently of both claims and beliefs. In the context of the commitment to the kind of explanatory relation between those activities and those contents mentioned above, this approach takes the form of a linguistic pragmatism that might take as its slogan Sellars's principle that *grasping a concept is mastering the use of a word*. James and Dewey were pragmatists in the sense I have picked out, since they try to understand conceptual content in terms of practices of using concepts. But, in line with their generally assimilationist approach to concept use, they were not specifically *linguistic* pragmatists. The later Wittgenstein, Quine, and Sellars (as well as Dummett and Davidson) are linguistic pragmatists, whose strategy of coming at the meaning of expressions by considering their use provides a counterbalance to the Frege-Russell-Carnap-Tarski platonistic model-theoretic approach to meaning.

4. The Genus of Conceptual Activity: *Representation* or *Expression?*

Besides this issue about the original *locus* of the conceptual, there is an issue about how to understand the *genus* of which it is a species. (As I have indicated, this is no less urgent for theories that concern themselves in the first instance with what is distinctive of the conceptual species of that genus than it is for those adopting the assimilationist order of proceeding.) The master concept of Enlightenment epistemology and semantics, at least since Descartes, was *representation*. Awareness was understood in representational terms—whether taking the form of direct awareness of representings or of indirect awareness of representeds via representations of them. Typically, specifically conceptual representations were taken to be just one kind of representation of which and by means of which we can be aware. This orienting thought remains active to this day, surviving the quite substantial transformations required, for instance, for naturalistic and broadly functional accounts of awareness by and of representations. The result is a familiar, arguably dominant, contemporary research program: to put in place a general conception of representation, the simpler forms of which are exhibited already in the activity of non–concept-using creatures, and on that basis elaborate ever more complex forms until one reaches something recognizable as specifically *conceptual* representation.

This representational paradigm[3] of what mindedness consists in is sufficiently ubiquitous that it is perhaps not easy to think of alternatives of similar generality and promise. One prominent countertradition, however, looks to the notion of *expression,* rather than representation, for the genus within which distinctively conceptual activity can become intelligible as a species.

To the Enlightenment picture of mind as *mirror*, Romanticism opposed an image of the mind as *lamp*.[4] Broadly cognitive activity was to be seen not as a kind of passive reflection but as a kind of active revelation. Emphasizing the importance of experimental intervention and the creative character of theory production motivated an assimilation of scientific to artistic activity, of finding as constrained making—a picture of knowing nature as producing a second nature (to use Leonardo da Vinci's phrase).

The sort of expressivism Herder initiated takes as its initial point of departure the process by which inner becomes outer when a feeling is expressed by a gesture.[5] We are then invited to consider more complex cases in which attitudes are expressed in actions, for instance, when a desire or intention issues in a corresponding doing, or a belief in saying. So long as we focus on the simplest cases, an expressivist model will not seem to offer a particularly promising avenue for construing the genus of which conceptual activity is a species (though one might say the same of the representational model if attention is focused on, say, the imprint of a seal on a wax tablet). But a suitable commentary on the model may be able to repair this impression somewhat.

First, we might think of the process of expression in the more complex and interesting cases as a matter not of transforming what is inner into what is outer but of making *explicit* what is *implicit*. This can be understood in a pragmatist sense of turning something we can initially only *do* into something we can *say:* codifying some sort of knowing *how* in the form of a knowing *that*. Second, as is suggested by this characterization of a pragmatist form of expressivism, in the cases of most interest in the present context, the notion of explicitness will be a *conceptual* one. The process of explicitation is to be the process of applying concepts: conceptualizing some subject matter. Third, we need not yield to the temptation, offered by the primitive expressive relation of gesture to feeling, to think of what is expressed and the expression of it as individually intelligible independently of consideration of the relation between them. At least in the more interesting cases, specification of what is implicit may depend on the possibility of making it explicit. And the explicit may not be specifiable apart from consideration of what is made explicit. On such a view, what is expressed must be understood in terms of the possibility of expressing it. Such a *relational* expressivism will understand linguistic performances and the intentional states they express each as essential elements in a whole that is intelligible only in terms of their relation. According to such an approach, for instance, one ought not to think that one can understand either believing or asserting except by abstracting from their role in the process of asserting what one believes (that is, this sort of expressivism has as a consequence a relational linguistic view of the layout of the conceptual realm).

Understanding the genus of which the conceptual is a species in representational terms invites a platonist order of explanation. That it does not demand one is clear from the possibility of psychologically or linguistically functionalist accounts of representational content. Nonetheless, expressivism is particularly congenial to a pragmatist order of semantic explanation, as is indicated by the formulation of the relation between what is implicit and what is explicit in terms of the distinction between knowing how and knowing that. The account presented in the body of this work is one kind of constitutive, pragmatist, relationally linguistic, conceptual expressivism. The commitment to trying to make expressivism work as a framework within which to understand concept use and (so) conceptual content sets this project off from most others on the contemporary scene. For a representational paradigm reigns not only in the whole spectrum of analytically pursued semantics, from model-theoretic, through possible worlds, directly counterfactual, and informational approaches to teleosemantic ones, but also in structuralism inheriting the broad outlines of Saussure's semantics, and even in those later continental thinkers whose poststructuralism is still so far mired in the representational paradigm that it can see no other alternative to understanding meaning in terms of signifiers standing for signifieds than to understand it in terms of signifiers standing for other signifiers. Even contemporary forms of pragmatism, which are explicitly motivated by the rejection of platonist forms of the representational paradigm, have not embraced or sought to develop an expressivist alternative.

5. Distinguishing the Conceptual: *Intensionalism* or *Inferentialism*?

I am not in this introduction pretending to argue for any of the methodological commitments I am rehearsing. My aim is to offer a quick sketch of the terrain against the background of which the approach pursued in the body of this work (and at greater length and in greater detail in *Making It Explicit*) takes its characteristic shape—to introduce and place those commitments, rather than so much as to begin to entitle myself to any of them. I said at the outset that I am particularly interested in what *distinguishes* the conceptual from the nonconceptual. This is not a topic that has attracted as much philosophical attention in contemporary circles as I think it deserves. Insofar as there is a consensus answer abroad, I think it must be that the conceptual (or the intentional) is distinguished by a special sort of intensionality: intersubstitution of coreferential or coextensional expressions or concepts does not preserve the content of ascriptions of intentional states, paradigmatically propositional attitudes such as thought and belief. (This is a datum that is relatively independent of how that content is construed, whether in representational terms of truth conditions or of propositions as sets of possible worlds, or as functional roles of some sort, in information-theoretic terms, assertibility conditions, and so on.) Quite a different approach is pursued here.

The master idea that animates and orients this enterprise is that what distinguishes specifically *discursive* practices from the doings of non–concept-using creatures is their *inferential* articulation. To talk about concepts is to talk about roles in reasoning. The original Romantic expressivists were (like the pragmatists, both classical and contemporary) *assimilationists* about the conceptual. My way of working out an expressivist approach is *exceptionalist,* focusing on the differentiae distinctive of the conceptual as such. It is a *rationalist* pragmatism, in giving pride of place to practices of giving and asking for reasons, understanding them as conferring conceptual content on performances, expressions, and states suitably caught up in those practices. In this way it differs from the view of other prominent theorists who are pragmatists in the sense of subscribing to use theorists of meaning such as Dewey, Heidegger, Wittgenstein, Dummett, and Quine. And it is a rationalist expressivism in that it understands *expressing* something, making it *explicit,* as putting it in a form in which it can both serve as and stand in need of *reasons:* a form in which it can serve as both premise and conclusion in *inferences.* Saying or thinking *that* things are thus-and-so is undertaking a distinctive kind of *inferentially* articulated commitment: putting it forward as a fit premise for further inferences, that is, *authorizing* its use as such a premise, and undertaking *responsibility* to entitle oneself to that commitment, to vindicate one's authority, under suitable circumstances, paradigmatically by exhibiting it as the conclusion of an inference from other such commitments to which one is or can become entitled. Grasping the *concept* that is applied in such a making explicit is mastering its *inferential* use: knowing (in the practical sense of being able to distinguish, a kind of knowing *how*) what else one would be committing oneself to by applying the concept, what would entitle one to do so, and what would preclude such entitlement.

What might be thought of as Frege's fundamental *pragmatic* principle is that in *asserting* a claim, one is committing oneself to its *truth*. The standard way of exploiting this principle is a platonist one: some grip on the concept of *truth* derived from one's semantic theory is assumed, and an account of the pragmatic force or speech act of assertion is elaborated based on this connection. But the principle can be exploited in more than one way, and linguistic pragmatism reverses the platonist order of explanation. Starting with an account of what one is *doing* in making a claim, it seeks to elaborate from it an account of what is *said,* the content or proposition—something that can be thought of in terms of truth conditions—to which one commits oneself by such a speech act.

What might be thought of as Frege's fundamental *semantic* principle is that a good inference never leads from a true claim(able) to one that is not true. It, too, can be exploited in either of two reductive orders of explanation.[6] The standard way is to assume that one has a prior grip on the notion of truth, and use it to explain what good inference consists in. Rationalist or inferentialist pragmatism reverses this order of explanation also. It starts with a practical distinction between good and bad inferences, understood as a distinction between appropriate and inappropriate *doings,* and goes on to understand talk about truth as talk about what is preserved by the good moves.

6. *Bottom-up* or *Top-down* Semantic Explanation?

According to such an inferentialist line of thought, the fundamental form of the conceptual is the *propositional,* and the core of concept use is applying concepts in propositionally contentful *assertions, beliefs,* and *thoughts.* It claims that to be propositionally contentful is to be able to play the basic inferential roles of both premise and conclusion in inferences. Demarcating the conceptual realm by appeal to inference accordingly involves coming down firmly on one side of another abstract methodological divide. For it entails treating the sort of conceptual content that is expressed by whole declarative sentences as prior in the order of explanation to the sort of content that is expressed by subsentential expressions such as singular terms and predicates. Traditional term logics built up from below, offering first accounts of the meanings of the concepts associated with singular and general terms (in a nominalistic representational way: in terms of what they name or stand for), then of *judgments* constructed by relating those terms, and finally of proprieties of *inferences* relating those judgments. This order of explanation is still typical of contemporary representational approaches to semantics (paradigmatically Tarskian model-theoretic ones). There are, however, platonistic representational semantic theories that begin by assigning semantic interpretants (for instance, sets of possible worlds) to declarative sentences. Pragmatist semantic theories typically adopt a top-down approach because they start from the *use* of concepts, and what one does with concepts is apply them in judgment and action. Thus Kant takes the judgment to be the minimal unit of experience (and so of awareness in his discursive sense) because it is the first element in the traditional logical hierarchy that one can take *responsibility* for. (Naming is not a doing that makes one *answerable* to anything.) Frege starts with judgeable conceptual contents because that is what pragmatic *force* can attach to. And Wittgenstein's focus on use leads him to privilege sentences as bits of language the utterance of which can make a move in a language game. I take these to be three ways of making essentially the same pragmatist point about the priority of the propositional. Again, the connection between propositionalism and pragmatism in the broad sense of approaching meaning from the side of use is not a coercive one, since a functionalist version of this approach might privilege contents associated with subsentential expressions. Inferentialism, however, is an essentially propositional doctrine.

In this respect, inferentialism and expressivism dovetail neatly. For the paradigm of expression is *saying* something. And what can play the role of premise and conclusion of inference is a saying in the sense of a *claiming*. Expressivism, like inferentialism, directs our attention in the first place to *propositional* conceptual contents. A further story must then be told about the *de*composition of such contents into the sort of conceptual contents that are expressed (in a derivative sense) by subsentential expressions such as singular terms and predicates. (And about their subsequent *re*composition to produce novel contents. Such a story is presented in Chapter 4.) Representationalism, by contrast, is motivated by a designational paradigm: the relation of a name to its bearer. In one standard way of pursuing this direction of explanation, one must then introduce a special ontological category of states of affairs, thought of as being represented by declarative sentences in something like the same way that objects are represented by singular terms.

Rationalist expressivism understands the explicit (the sayable in the sense of claimable, the form something must be in to count as having been expressed) in terms of its inferential role. Coupled with a linguistic pragmatism, such a view entails that practices of giving and asking for reasons have a privileged, indeed defining, role with respect to linguistic practice generally. What makes something a specifically *linguistic* (and therefore, according to this view, discursive) practice is that it accords some performances the force or significance of *claimings,* of *propositionally* contentful commitments, which can both serve as and stand in need of reasons. Practices that do not involve reasoning are not linguistic or (therefore) discursive practices. Thus the 'Slab' *Sprachspiel* that Wittgenstein introduces in the opening sections of the *Philosophical Investigations* should not, by these standards of demarcation, count as a genuine *Sprach*spiel. It is a *vocal* but not yet a *verbal* practice. By contrast to Wittgenstein, the inferential identification of the conceptual claims that language (discursive practice) has a *center;* it is not a motley. Inferential practices of producing and consuming *reasons* are *downtown* in the region of linguistic practice. Suburban linguistic practices utilize and depend on the conceptual contents forged in the game of giving and asking for reasons, are parasitic on it. Claiming, being able to justify one's claims, and using one's claims to justify other claims and actions are not just one among other sets of things one can do with language. They are not on a par with other 'games' one can play. They are what in the first place make possible talking, and therefore thinking: sapience in general. Of course we do *many* other things as concept users besides applying concepts in judgment and action and justifying those applications. But (by contrast to the indiscriminately egalitarian picture presented by contemporary neo-Romantic theorists such as Derrida) according to this sort of semantic rationalism, those sophisticated, latecoming linguistic and more generally discursive activities are intelligible in principle only against the background of the core practices of inference-and-assertion.

7. *Atomism* or *Holism?*

Closely related to the issue of top-down or bottom-up semantic explanation is the issue of semantic *holism* versus semantic *atomism*. The tradition of formal semantics has been resolutely atomistic, in the sense that the assignment of a semantic interpretant to one element (say, a proper name) is taken to be intelligible independently of the assignment of semantic interpretants to any other elements (for instance, predicates or other proper names). One does not need to know anything about what other dots represent, or what blue wavy lines represent, in order to understand that a particular dot stands for Cleveland on a map. The task of formal semantics is the bottom-up one of explaining how semantically relevant whatsits can systematically be assigned to complex expressions, given that they have been assigned already to simple ones. Atomism adds that the assignments to the simple ones can be done one by one. By contrast, inferentialist semantics is resolutely *holist*. On an inferentialist account of conceptual content, one cannot have *any* concepts unless one has *many* concepts. For the content of each concept is articulated by its inferential relations to *other* concepts. Concepts, then, must come in packages (though it does not yet follow that they must come in just one great big one). Conceptual holism is not a commitment that one might be motivated to undertake independently of the considerations that lead one to an inferential conception of the conceptual. It is rather a straightforward consequence of that approach.

8. *Traditional* or *Rationalist* Expressivism?

The heart of any expressivist theory is of course its account of expressing. What is expressed appears in two forms, as implicit (only potentially expressible) and explicit (actually expressed). To talk of expression is to talk about a process of transformation of what in virtue of its role in that process becomes visible as a *content* that appears in two *forms*, as implicit and then as explicit. As I indicated above, traditional Romantic expressivism took as its paradigm something like the relationship between an inner *feeling* expressed by an outer *gesture*. The *rationalist expressivism* informing the present account is quite different. Where, as here, explicitness is identified with specifically *conceptual* articulation, expressing something is *conceptualizing* it: putting it into conceptual form. I said at the outset that the goal of the enterprise is a clear account of sapient awareness, of the sense in which being aware of something is bringing it under a concept. On the approach pursued here, doing that is making a claim or judgment about what one is (thereby) aware of, forming a belief about it— in general, addressing it in a form that can serve as and stand in need of reasons, making it *inferentially* significant. The image of conceptualizing the unconceptualized is a familiar focus of philosophical attention, and it has given rise to a familiar panoply of philosophical pathologies. The rationalist expressivist course pursued here is distinguished by the particular strategy it employs for understanding the relation between the merely implicit and the conceptually explicit.

That strategy depends on a constellation of related inferentialist ideas. The first and most fundamental idea, already mentioned above, is a way of thinking about conceptual explicitness. To be explicit in the conceptual sense is to play a specifically *inferential* role. In the most basic case, it is to be *propositionally* contentful in the sense of being fit to serve both as a premise and as a conclusion in inferences. According to the relational linguistic view, to be thinkable or believable in this sense is to be *assertible*. The basic way of working out the pragmatist explanatory strategy is to understand *saying* (thinking, believing . . .) *that* such and such (that is, adopting a *propositionally contentful* attitude) in terms of a distinctive kind of knowing *how* or being able to *do* something. Inferentialism picks out the relevant sort of doing by its *inferential* articulation. Propositional (and more generally conceptual) contents become available to those engaging in linguistic practices, whose core is drawing conclusions and offering justifications. Merely reliably responding differentially to red things is not yet being *aware* of them *as* red. Discrimination by producing repeatable responses (as a machine or a pigeon might do) sorts the eliciting stimuli, and in that sense classifies them. But it is not yet *conceptual* classification, and so involves no awareness of the sort under investigation here. (If instead of teaching a pigeon to peck one button rather than another under appropriate sensory stimulation, we teach a parrot to utter one noise rather than another, we get only to the vocal, not yet to the verbal.) As a next stage, we might imagine a normative practice, according to which red things are *appropriately* responded to by making a certain noise. That would still not be a conceptual matter. What is *implicit* in that sort of practical doing becomes *explicit* in the application of the *concept red* when that responsive capacity or skill is put into a larger context that includes treating the responses as inferentially significant: as providing reasons for making other moves in the language game, and as themselves potentially standing in need of reasons that could be provided by making still other moves. The first advantage that this rationalist pragmatism claims over earlier forms of expressivism is provided by this relatively clear inferential notion of conceptual explicitness.

Pragmatism about the conceptual seeks to understand what it is explicitly to *say* or *think that* something is the case in terms of what one must implicitly know *how* (be able) to *do*. That the relevant sort of doing is a constellation of asserting and inferring, making claims and giving and asking for reasons for them, is the essence of rationalist or inferentialist pragmatism about the conceptual. But once such an inferential notion of explicitness (propositional or, more generally, conceptual contentfulness) has been put in place, we can appeal to this notion of expressing (what is explicit) to understand various senses in which something can be expressed (what is implicit). The inferentialist picture actually puts in play several notions of implicitness. The first is what is made explicit by a claim or becomes explicit in it: a proposition, possible fact, what is said (sayable) or thought or believed. But in another sense we can talk about what still remains implicit in an explicit claim, namely, its inferential consequences. For in the context of a constellation of inferential practices, endorsing or committing oneself to one proposition (claimable) is implicitly endorsing or committing oneself to others which follow from it. Mastery of these inferential connections is the implicit background against which alone explicit claiming is intelligible. Actually drawing inferences from an explicit claimable (something that can be said, thought, and so on) is exploring the inferential relations that articulate its content. Since in *saying* that things are thus-and-so, for instance, that the cloth is red, one is not in the same sense *saying* (making explicit) that it is colored and spatially extended, those consequences count as only implicit. Since they articulate the content of the original saying, they are at least implicit in it. 'Implicit' is once again given a relatively clear inferential sense, but one that is distinct from the sense in which the fact that the cloth is red (to which one can reliably respond differentially) is made explicit in the claim. In different but related senses, an explicit claim has implicit in it:

1. proprieties governing inferential moves to and from the commitments to the claimable content in question;
2. the other claims that are inferential consequences of the first one, according to the practical proprieties mentioned in (1); and
3. the conceptual content of the claim, which is articulated by the inferences in (1).

These notions of implicitness are direct products of the basic inferential model of explicitness.

9. Is the Semantic Task of Logic Epistemological or Expressive?

One standard way to think of logic is as giving us special epistemic access to a kind of truth. Logic is for establishing the truth of certain kinds of claims, by *proving* them. But logic can also be thought of in expressive terms, as a distinctive set of tools for *saying* something that cannot otherwise be made explicit. Seeing how this can be so depends on making a further move: applying the original model of explicitness to the inferential consequences that are implicit (in the sense just considered) in any explicit claim. According to the inferentialist account of concept use, in making a claim one is implicitly endorsing a set of inferences, which articulate its conceptual content. Implicitly endorsing those inferences is a sort of doing. Understanding the conceptual content to which one has committed oneself is a kind of practical mastery: a bit of know-how that consists in being able to discriminate what does and does not follow from the claim, what would be evidence for and against it, and so on. Making explicit that know-how, the inferences one has implicitly endorsed, is putting it in the form of a claim *that* things are thus-and-so. In this case a central expressive resource for doing that is provided by basic *logical* vocabulary. In applying the concept *lion* to Leo, I implicitly commit myself to the applicability of the concept *mammal* to him. If my language is expressively rich enough to contain *conditionals,* I can say that *if* Leo is a lion, *then* Leo is a mammal. (And if the language is expressively rich enough to include quantificational operators, I can say that if *anything* is a lion, then it is a mammal.) That Cleo is a cephalopod is good (indeed, decisive) evidence that she is not a lion. If my language is expressively rich enough to contain *negation,* I can make that implicit inferential component articulating the content of the concept *lion* explicit by saying that *if* Cleo is a cephalopod, then Cleo is *not* a mammal.

By saying things like this, by using *logical* vocabulary, I can make explicit the implicit inferential commitments that articulate the content of the concepts I apply in making ordinary explicit claims. Here the original inferential-propositional model of awareness (in the sense of sapience) is applied at a higher level. In the first application, we get an account of *consciousness*—for example, *that* Leo is a lion. In the second application we get an account of a kind of semantic *self*-consciousness. For in this way we begin to *say* what we are *doing* in *saying* that Leo is a lion. For instance, we make explicit (in the form of a claimable, and so propositional content) that we are committing ourselves thereby to his being a mammal by saying *that* if something is a lion, then it is a mammal. An account along these lines of the expressive role distinctive of logical vocabulary as such is introduced in Chapter 1 of this book. It is applied and extended in subsequent chapters to include such sophisticated locutions as normative vocabulary (in Chapter 2) and intentional tropes such as some uses of 'of' and 'about' (in Chapter 5), which are not usually put in a box with conditionals and negation. Inferentialism about conceptual content in this way makes possible a new kind of expressivism about logic. Applying the inferential model of explicitness, and so of expression, to the functioning of logical vocabulary provides a proving ground for the model that permits its elaboration at a level of clarity and exactness that has (to say the least) been unusual within the expressivist tradition. Two dimensions along which philosophical payoffs can be expected from this fact are explored in Chapters 4 and 5, which present an expressive account of the nature and deduction of the necessity of the use of singular terms (and predicates), and an account of the expressive role characteristic of explicitly intentional and representational vocabulary, respectively.

Conditional claims—and claims formed by the use of logical vocabulary in general, of which the conditional is paradigmatic for the inferentialist—express a kind of semantic self-consciousness because they make explicit the inferential relations, consequences, and contents of ordinary nonlogical claims and concepts. It is possible to use the model of (partial) logical explicitation of nonlogical conceptual contents to illuminate certain features of ordinary making explicit in nonlogical claims. For instance, the conceptual content of a concept such as *red* has as a crucial element its *non*inferential circumstances of appropriate application (which, recall, are appealed to in the *broadly* inferential notion of content, since in applying the concept, one implicitly endorses the propriety of the inference from the concept's circumstances of appropriate application to its consequences of application, regardless of whether those circumstances are themselves specified in narrowly inferential terms). Part of the practical skill that forms the implicit background of knowing how against which alone a broadly inferentialist semantic theory can explain the practice of explicitly claiming that something is red, then, is the capacity noninferentially to respond appropriately and differentially to red things. Chapter 3 discusses how this part of the implicit background of explicit application of concepts of observables can itself be made explicit, in the logical sense, by first tracking it with a corresponding *reliability inference* and then codifying that inference with a conditional. In inferentialist terms, the reliability inference *conceptualizes* the initially nonconceptual capacity to respond differentially to red things. Once it appears in this inferential guise, the aspect of the content of the concept *red* that is still implicit (in another sense) even when presented in the form of a reliability inference can be made explicit by using a conditional, just as for any other inferentially articulated aspect.

This development of the relation of expression between what is explicit and what is implicit is guided throughout by the fundamental idea of demarcating the conceptual by its specifically inferential articulation. At the first stage, that idea yields an understanding of the end result of making something explicit in a claimable (judgeable, thinkable, believable), that is, propositional content, of the sort expressed by the use of basic declarative sentences. At the second stage, the same inferentialist idea leads to an expressive model of the conceptual role distinctive of logical vocabulary, which serves to make explicit in the form of claimables (paradigmatically, conditional ones) the inferential relations that implicitly articulate the contents of the ordinary nonlogical concepts we use in making things explicit in the sense specified at the first stage. At the third stage, the notion of the expressive relation between what is explicit and what is implicit that was developed at the second stage in connection with the use of distinctively logical concepts is applied to illuminate further the relation between what is explicit in the sense of the first stage and what is made explicit thereby. The result is an account with a structure recognizable as Hegelian: a rationalist, expressivist account of (a kind of) consciousness (namely, sapient awareness) provides the basis for a corresponding account of (a kind of) self-consciousness (namely, semantic or conceptual self-consciousness), which is then called upon to deepen the original story by providing a model for understanding the sort of consciousness with which the account began.

II. Historical Context: Rationalism, Pragmatism, and Expressivism

At the very center of this account is its *rationalism:* the pride of place it gives to specifically *inferential* articulation, to playing a role in practices of giving and asking for *reasons*. It provides the answer I offer to the question how to demarcate the distinctive realm of the *conceptual*. Specifically *linguistic* practice is picked out (and recognized as discursive) by its incorporation of inferential-and-assertional practices: attributing and undertaking commitments to the propriety of making certain moves and occupying certain positions whose contents are determined by their places in those practices. The resulting *rationalistic pragmatism* is importantly different in just this respect from that of other semantic pragmatists such as Dewey, Heidegger, Wittgenstein, Quine, and Rorty. Again, *rationalistic expressivism* has important conceptual resources and advantages denied to traditional Romantic expressivism. This version of expressivism offers a framework within which it is possible to do detailed semantic work (the argument presented in Chapter 4 is emblematic). And that same framework makes possible an expressivist approach to *logic,* which provides potentially important new insights—for instance, into the expressive role distinctive of *normative* vocabulary (discussed in Chapter 2), and the expressive role distinctive of *intentional* or explicitly *representational* vocabulary (discussed in Chapter 5).

Empiricism has been the fighting faith and organizing principle of philosophy in the English-speaking world since at least the time of Locke. Its distinctive twentieth-century form, developed by thinkers such as Russell, Carnap, and Quine, joins to the classical insistence on the origin of knowledge in *experience* an emphasis on the crucial cognitive role played by *language* and *logic.* A central goal of this book is to introduce a way of thinking about these latter topics—and so about meaning, mind, and knowledge—that swings free of the context of empiricist commitments that has shaped discussion within this tradition.

In turning away from empiricism I do not mean to deny that consideration of perceptual practices must play a crucial role in our epistemology and semantics. What might be called *platitudinous empiricism* restricts itself to the observations that without perceptual experience we can have no knowledge of contingent matters of fact, and more deeply, that conceptual content is unintelligible apart from its relation to perceptual experience.[7] These are not controversial claims. (Indeed, I think it is very difficult to find any philosophers who have *ever* disputed them, including the most notorious candidates. But I will not try to support that claim here.) The theoretical and explanatory commitments of philosophically substantial empiricisms go well beyond these platitudes. My main target is the semantic theory that I see as underlying empiricist approaches to meaning, mind, knowledge, and action. Empiricism is a current of thought too broad and multifarious, with too many shifting eddies, backwaters, and side channels, to be confined within the well-defined banks of necessary and sufficient conditions. Its general course, though, is marked out by commitment to grounding theoretical and practical reasoning and concept use in the occurrence of episodes we immediately find ourselves with: sense experiences on the cognitive side, and felt motivations or preferences on the active side. In the forms I find most objectionable, having these experiences is thought of as not requiring the exercise of specifically *conceptual* abilities. It is understood rather as a *pre*conceptual capacity shareable with non–concept-using mammals. Its deliverances are accordingly conceived of as available to explain what concept use consists in, and as providing the raw materials conceptual activities work on or with. (Traditional abstractionist and associationist strategies are just particular ways of working out this line of thought; many others are possible.)

Classical empiricist philosophy of mind takes immediate perceptual experiences as the paradigm of awareness or consciousness. Classical empiricist epistemology takes as its paradigm of empirical knowledge those same experiences, to which it traces the warrant for and authority of all the rest. As the tradition has developed, it has become clearer that both rest on a more or less explicit semantic picture, according to which the content of experience, awareness, and knowledge is to be understood in the first instance in *representational* terms: as a matter of what is (or pur-

ports to be) represent*ed* by some represent*ing* states or episodes. In contemporary incarnations, this notion of representational content is most often unpacked in terms of what objects,
events, or states of affairs actually causally elicited the representation, or which ones would reliably elicit representations of that
kind under various conditions. This way of thinking about the
content of empirical knowledge, to begin with perceptual experience, is then naturally seen to be complemented by a philosophy
of language that focuses on reference, denotation, and extension,
following the pattern of extensional model-theoretic semantics
for the language of first-order predicate logic.

Empiricism attempts to understand the content of concepts in
terms of the origin of empirical beliefs in experience that we just
find ourselves with, and the origin of practical intentions in desires
or preferences that in the most basic case we just find ourselves
with. The *rationalist* order of explanation understands concepts as
norms determining what counts as a *reason* for particular beliefs,
claims, and intentions, whose content is articulated by the application of those concepts and which such statuses can be reasons for.
Its impetus is a classically rationalist thought, which Sellars (in an
autobiographical sketch) says motivated his philosophical development starting already in the 1930s: the thought that "what was
needed was a functional theory of concepts which would make
their role in reasoning, rather than supposed origin in experience,
their primary feature."[8] The difference is most telling when we ask
about the relation between awareness and concept use. The empiricist understands concept use as an achievement to be understood against the background of a prior sort of awareness, which
justifies or makes appropriate the application of one concept rather
than another. To play this latter role, the awareness in question
must amount to something more than just the reliable differential
responsiveness of merely irritable devices such as land mines and
pressure plates that open doors in supermarkets. For the rationalist, on the contrary, awareness of the sort that has a potentially

normative significance (the genus of which cognitive significance is a species) consists in the application of concepts. One must already have concepts to be aware in this sense. Of course, this immediately raises the question how one could come to be a concept user unless one could already be aware of things. But to this a pragmatist such as Sellars can reply with a story about how initially merely differentially responsive creatures can be initiated into the implicitly normative social practice of giving and asking for reasons, so that some of their responses can come to count as or have the social significance of endorsements, of the making or staking of inferentially articulated *claims.*[9]

Besides rejecting empiricism, the rationalist pragmatism and expressivism presented here is opposed to *naturalism,* at least as that term is usually understood. For it emphasizes what distinguishes discursive creatures, as subject to distinctively conceptual norms, from their non–concept-using ancestors and cousins. Conceptual norms are brought into play by social linguistic practices of giving and asking for reasons, of assessing the propriety of claims and inferences. Products of *social* interactions (in a strict sense that distinguishes them merely from features of populations) are not studied by the *natural* sciences—though they are not for that reason to be treated as spooky and *super*natural. In conferring conceptual content on performances, states, and expressions suitably caught up in them, those practices institute a realm of *culture* that rests on, but goes beyond, the background of reliable differential responsive dispositions and their exercise characteristic of merely natural creatures. Once concept use is on the scene, a distinction opens up between things that have *natures* and things that have *histories.* Physical things such as electrons and aromatic compounds would be paradigmatic of the first class, while cultural formations such as English Romantic poetry and uses of the terms 'nature' and 'natural' would be paradigmatic of the second.

The relations between these categories is a complex affair. Physical, chemical, and biological *things* have natures rather than histories, but what about the disciplines that define and study them? Should physics itself be thought of as something that has a nature, or as something that has a history? Concluding the latter is giving a certain kind of pride of place to the historical, cultural, and conceptual. For it is in effect treating the *distinction* between things that have natures and things that have histories, between things studied by the *Naturwissenschaften* and things studied by the *Geisteswissenschaften,* as itself a cultural formation: the sort of thing that itself has a history rather than a nature. Grasping a concept is mastering the use of a word—and uses of words are a paradigm of the sort of thing that must be understood historically. In this sense even concepts such as *electron* and *aromatic compound* are the sort of thing that has a history. But they are not *purely* historical. For the proprieties governing the application of those concepts depend on what inferences involving them are *correct,* that is, on what *really* follows from what. And that depends on how things are with electrons and aromatic compounds, not just on what judgments and inferences we endorse. (To say that is to say that our *use* of the corresponding words should not be thought of as restricted to our dispositions to such endorsements.) Understanding the relevant sort of dependence—the way what inferences are correct, and so what we are really committing ourselves to by applying them, and so what their contents really are (the contents we have conferred on them by using them as we do), as opposed to what we take them to be—is a delicate and important task. Some essential raw materials for it are assembled in the final three chapters of this book. Chapter 4 offers an account of what it is to talk about *objects.* Chapter 5 tells what it is to take our talk to be *about* objects. And Chapter 6 shows how the structure of reasoning makes it possible to understand subjecting our claims to assessments according to a kind of correctness in which authority is invested in the things we are talking about rather than in our attitudes toward them. None of these is a naturalistic account.

In addition to rejecting empiricism and embracing nonnaturalism, the rationalistic semantic theory introduced here is unusual in not taking *representation* as its fundamental concept. A methodological commitment to beginning an account of concept use (and so, eventually, of conceptual content) with reasoning rather than representing does not require denying that there is an important representational dimension to concept use. Indeed, the unusual explanatory starting point has the advantage of bringing into relief certain features of conceptual representation that are hard to notice otherwise. The final three chapters highlight some of these, while beginning the process of cashing the promissory note issued by an inferentialist order of explanation—that is, offering an account of *referential* relations to objects in terms ultimately of *inferential* relations among claims. Of course, *non*inferential language entry moves in perception and language exit moves in action play a crucial role in the story too. But the specifically *inferential* articulation of the acknowledgments of propositional commitments that result from observation and result in intentional performances are to the fore in understanding the cognitive and practical *normative* significance of the reliable differential responsive capacities exercised in those processes.

I call the view that inferential articulation is a *necessary* element in the demarcation of the conceptual '*weak* inferentialism'. The view that inferential articulation *broadly construed* is *sufficient* to account for conceptual content I call '*strong* inferentialism'. The view that inferential articulation *narrowly* construed is *sufficient* to account for conceptual content, I call '*hyper*inferentialism'. The difference between the broad and the narrow construal of inferential articulation is just whether or not *non*inferential circumstances of application (in the case of concepts such as *red* that have noninferential reporting uses) and consequences of application (in the case of concepts such as *ought* that have noninferential practical uses) are taken into account. The broad sense focuses attention on the inferential commitment that is implicitly undertaken in using any concept whatever, even those with noninferential circumstances or consequences of application: the commitment, namely, to the propriety of the inference from the circumstances to the consequences of application. The view endorsed here is strong inferentialism.[10]

Inferentialism of any sort is committed to a certain kind of semantic *holism*, as opposed to the *atomism* that often goes hand in hand with commitment to a representationalist order of semantic explanation. For if the conceptual content expressed by each sentence or word is understood as essentially consisting in its inferential relations (broadly construed) or articulated by its inferential relations (narrowly construed), then one must grasp many such contents in order to grasp any. Such holistic conceptual role approaches to semantics potentially face problems concerning both the *stability* of conceptual contents under change of belief and commitment to the propriety of various inferences, and the possibility of *communication* between individuals who endorse different claims and inferences. Such concerns are rendered much less urgent, however, if one thinks of concepts as *norms* determining the *correctness* of various moves. The norms I am binding myself to by using the term 'molybdenum'—what actually follows from or is incompatible with the applicability of the concept— need not change as my views about molybdenum and its inferential surround change. And you and I may be bound by just the same public linguistic and conceptual norms in the vicinity in spite of the fact that we are disposed to make different claims and inferential moves. It is up to me whether I play a token of the 'molybdenum' type in the game of giving and asking for reasons. But it is not then up to me what the significance of that move is. (And I do not take the case to be significantly different if I play such a token internally, in thought.)

As I have already remarked, inferentialism also carries with it a commitment to the conceptual primacy of the *propositional*. Thus inferentialism semantic explanations reverse the traditional order:

beginning with proprieties of inference, they explain propositional content, and in terms of both go on to explain the conceptual content expressed by subsentential expressions such as singular terms and predicates. Chapter 4 describes how this last step (which has not been much attended to by recent inferentialists such as Sellars and—on my reading—Dummett) might be accomplished.

The rationalist form of expressivism pursued here also involves rejecting conventional wisdom about the nature and philosophical significance of *logic*. Logic is not properly understood as the study of a distinctive kind of *formal* inference. It is rather the study of the inferential roles of vocabulary playing a distinctive *expressive* role: codifying in explicit form the inferences that are implicit in the use of ordinary, nonlogical vocabulary. Making explicit the inferential roles of the logical vocabulary then can take the form of presenting patterns of inference involving them that are formally valid in the sense that they are invariant under substitution of nonlogical for nonlogical vocabulary. But that task is subsidiary and instrumental only. The task of logic is in the first instance to help us *say* something about the conceptual contents expressed by the use of nonlogical vocabulary, not to *prove* something about the conceptual contents expressed by the use of logical vocabulary. On this picture, *formal* proprieties of inference essentially involving logical vocabulary derive from and must be explained in terms of *material* proprieties of inference essentially involving nonlogical vocabulary rather than the other way around. Logic is accordingly not a canon or standard of right reasoning. It can help us make explicit (and hence available for criticism and transformation) the inferential commitments that govern the use of all our vocabulary, and hence articulate the contents of all our concepts.

Finally, the views presented here turn on their head prevailing humean ideas about practical reasoning. According to this common approach—which is very much in evidence in Davidson's writings on action, and of rational-choice theorists and others who approach the norms of rationality through decision theory or game theory—the norms governing practical reasoning and defining rational action are essentially *instrumental* norms, which derive their authority from intrinsically motivating preferences or desires. Those states are the empiricist analogs, on the side of agency, to the preconceptual episodes of awareness to which epistemic authority is traced on the side of cognition. Chapter 2 offers an account in which statements about what an agent prefers or desires are interpreted instead as codifying commitment to certain specific patterns of practical reasoning, selected from among a wide variety of patterns that are codified by the use of other normative vocabulary. The concepts of desire and preference are accordingly demoted from their position of privilege, and take their place as having a derivative and provincial sort of normative authority. Endorsement and commitment are at the center of rational agency—as of rationality in general—and inclination enters only insofar as rational agents must bring inclination in the train of rational propriety, not the other way around.

So I am putting forward a view that is opposed to many (if not most) of the large theoretical, explanatory, and strategic commitments that have shaped and motivated Anglo-American philosophy in the twentieth century: empiricism, naturalism, representationalism, semantic atomism, formalism about logic, and instrumentalism about the norms of practical rationality. In spite of my disagreements with central elements of the worldview that has animated analytic philosophy, I take my expository and argumentative structure and the criteria of adequacy for having made a claim with a clear content, argued for it, and responsibly followed out its consequences resolutely from the Anglo-American tradition. I do not think those standards need be taken to entail or be warranted only by this one constellation of ideas. Indeed, although the enterprise I am engaged in here is not happily identified with *analysis of meanings* in a traditional sense, it is properly thought of as pursuing a recognizable successor project. For what

I am trying to do is in a clear and specific inferential sense make *explicit* what is *implicit* in various philosophically important concepts. Among the examples treated in the following pages are concepts such as *conceptual content, logic, ought, reliable, singular term,* what is expressed by the 'of' or 'about' of intentional directedness, and *objectivity.*

Sellars once said that the aim of his work as a whole was to begin moving analytic philosophy from its *humean* phase into a *kantian* one. The full implications of this remark include reverberations contributed by many of the chambers and corridors of the Kantian edifice. But at its heart, I think, is the conviction that the distinctive nature, contribution, and significance of the *conceptual* articulation of thought and action have been systematically slighted by empiricism in all its forms. Although the addition of logic to the mix in the twentieth century was a promising development, there was from Sellars's point of view a failure to rethink from the beginning the constraints and criteria of adequacy of the enterprise in the light of the expressive power the new formal idioms put at our disposal. The result was the pursuit of traditional empiricist visions by other means—ones that could not in principle do justice in the end to the normativity of concept use that finds its expression variously in the distinction between laws of nature codifying inferential relations among facts, on the one hand, and mere regularities regarding them, on the other, and in the difference between acting for a reason and merely moving when prompted. The more promising alternative is to focus to begin with on the conceptual articulation of perceptually acquired and practically pursued commitments and entitlements rather than on the experiences and inclinations with which we simply find ourselves. That kantian strategy is a better one for the same sort of reasons that lead us to expect that one will learn more about a building by studying blueprints than by studying bricks.

My teacher Richard Rorty has described the enterprise to which this volume is a contribution as an extension of Sellars's: to make possible a further transition from a *kantian* to a *hegelian* approach to thought and action.[11] The justice of this characterization can be understood in terms of the strategic options already rehearsed here. First, I am interested in the divide between *nature* and *culture*. In this context we can identify the realm of the cultural with activities that either consist in the application of concepts in judgment and action or that presuppose such capacities. The *Geisteswissenschaften* have as their proper aim the study of concept use and things made possible by it—activities of which only concept users are capable. One of my principal goals is to present and explore the consequences of a particular sort of principle of demarcation for the realm of culture, so understood. Although of course cultural activities arise within the framework of a natural world, I am most concerned with what is made possible by the emergence of the peculiar constellation of conceptually articulated comportments that Hegel called "Geist." Cultural products and activities become explicit as such only by the use of normative vocabulary that is in principle not reducible to the vocabulary of the natural sciences (though of course the same phenomena under other descriptions are available in that vocabulary). Indeed, the deployment of the vocabulary of the natural sciences (like that of any other vocabulary) is itself a cultural phenomenon, something that becomes intelligible only within the conceptual horizon provided by the *Geisteswissenschaften*. The study of natures itself has a history, and its own nature, if any, must be approached through the study of that history. This is a picture and an aspiration that we owe to Hegel.

A second dimension of Hegelian influence is his *pragmatism* about conceptual norms. One of Kant's great insights is that judgments and actions are to be distinguished from the responses of merely natural creatures by their distinctive *normative* status, as things we are in a distinctive sense *responsible* for. He understood *concepts* as the norms that determine just what we have made ourselves responsible for, what we have committed ourselves to and what would entitle us to it, by particular acts of judging and acting. Kant, however, punted many hard questions about the nature and origins of this normativity, of the bindingness of concepts, out of the familiar phenomenal realm of experience into the noumenal realm. Hegel brought these issues back to earth by understanding *normative* statuses as *social* statuses—by developing a view according to which (as my colleague John Haugeland put the point in another context)[12] *all transcendental constitution is social institution.* The background against which the conceptual activity of making things explicit is intelligible is taken to be implicitly normative essentially *social* practice.

Pragmatism about the norms implicit in cognitive activity came down to us in the first half of the twentieth century from three independent directions: from the classical American pragmatists, culminating in Dewey; from the Heidegger of *Being and Time;* and from the Wittgenstein of the *Philosophical Investigations.* In trying to work out how the insights of these traditions (partly common, partly complementary) could be applied to make progress within contemporary philosophy of language and philosophy of mind, however, I found myself driven back to Hegel's original version. For unlike all three of these more recent sorts of social practice theory, Hegel's is a *rationalist* pragmatism. By contrast to their conceptual assimilationism, he gives pride of place to *reasoning* in understanding what it is to say or do something.

Again, Dewey and James,[13] the early Heidegger, and the later Wittgenstein each resisted, in his own way, the *representational* semantic paradigm. But none of them evidently provides an alternative paradigm that is structurally rich enough and definite enough either to do real semantic work with—of the sort done by model-theoretic developments of representationalism, including possible worlds semantics[14]—or to provide an account of the distinctive function of *logical* vocabulary. Hegel's *rationalistic,* inferentialist version of the Romantic *expressivist* tradition he inherited, it seemed to me, holds out the promise of just such an alternative paradigm. Hegel's version of expressivism is further attractive in that it is not only pragmatic and inferentialist about the conceptual but also *relational,* in the sense that the implicit and the explicit are each at least in part constituted by their expressive relation to each other.[15] The inferentialist understanding of explicitness is just what is needed to make an expressive alternative to representationalism viable. As I put the point above, *rationalist* expressivism understands the *explicit*—the thinkable, the sayable, the form something must be in to count as having been *expressed*—in terms of its role in *inference*. I take Hegel to have introduced this idea, although he takes the minimal unit of conceptual content to be the whole holistic system of inferentially interrelated judgeables, and so is not a propositionalist.

Finally, this rationalist expressivist pragmatism forges a link between *logic* and *self-consciousness,* in the sense of making explicit the implicit background against which alone anything can be made explicit, that is recognizably Hegelian. For it offers an account of a kind of *consciousness,* awareness in the sense of *sapience,* which underwrites a corresponding account of a kind of *self*-consciousness: *semantic* or *conceptual* self-consciousness. This notion of what is made explicit by the characteristic use of specifically *logical* vocabulary then makes possible a new appreciation of the sort of consciousness with which the story begins.[16]

I think this is a constellation of ideas that has the prospect of enlarging the frontiers of contemporary analytic philosophy. My hope is that by slighting the similarities to animals which preoccupied Locke and Hume and highlighting the possibilities opened up by engaging in social practices of giving and asking for reasons, we will get closer to an account of being human that does justice to the kinds of consciousness and self-consciousness distinctive of us as *cultural,* and not merely *natural,* creatures.

III. Structure of the Book

The six chapters that make up the body of this work present ideas and arguments drawn from or developing out of my 1994 book *Making It Explicit.* There is nothing in them that will come as a surprise to anyone who has mastered that work. They were originally written as lectures, each intended to be intelligible in its own right, apart from its relation to the others. I had in mind audiences that had perhaps not so much as dipped into the big book but were curious about its themes and philosophical consequences. The lectures have been presented individually on many occasions, to many audiences, whose penetrating questions and lively discussion have helped me avoid at least some errors and to groom and streamline the presentations. The lectures were also written with an eye to mutual reinforcement and cumulative effect for those occasions when I was afforded the opportunity for a more extended presentation. I delivered versions of all but one (Chapter 3, on reliabilism) as the Townsend Lectures at Berkeley in the fall of 1997, and a different set of five (all but the last) more recently at the Goethe Universität in Frankfurt in the winter of 1999. The ancestors of Chapters 1, 4, and 5 saw the light of day as my Hempel Lectures at Princeton in the spring of 1994.[17] I think experience has proven that the stories told in each of these chapters can stand on their own, and that together they give a good picture of some of the argumentative high points of the approach to language and thought developed at length in *Making It Explicit*. Where questions arise about the presuppositions and context of these arguments, however, it should be kept in mind that that work is what should be consulted, and should be considered as offering the fullest account I can manage—including about the topics put on the table in this introduction. A number of important motivations, commitments, and developments have had to be omitted in this shorter, simpler book.

Chapter 1, "Semantic Inferentialism and Logical Expressivism," introduces and motivates two basic ideas. The first is that to have specifically *conceptual* content is to play a certain kind of role in *reasoning*. The most basic sort of conceptual content is *propositional* content: the sort of content expressed by declarative sentences (and the 'that' clauses or content-specifying sentential complements of propositional attitude ascriptions). Because contents of this sort are the right shape to be sayable, thinkable, and believable, they can be understood as making something *explicit.* The claim is that to have or express a content of this kind just is to be able to play the role both of premise and of conclusion in *inferences.* The second idea is that the expressive role characteristic of *logical* vocabulary as such is to make inferential relations explicit. Thus *conditionals* are treated as paradigms of logical locutions. This line of thought makes sense only if one thinks of proprieties of inference as extending beyond those underwritten by logical form. That is, one must acknowledge that besides inferences that are *formally* good in the sense of being *logically* valid, there are inferences that are *materially* good in the sense of articulating the contents of the *non*logical concepts applied in their premises and conclusions.

In the rest of the book these ideas are applied to shed light on a variety of philosophical issues: normativity and practical reasoning in Chapter 2, the ultimately inferential nature of appeals to the reliability of cognitive processes such as perception in Chapter 3, how the notion of substitution allows the inferential semantic approach to be extended to subsentential expressions (which cannot play the direct inferential role of premises and conclusions) such as singular terms and predicates in Chapter 4, the inferential expressive role characteristic of the locutions that make explicit the intentional directedness or representational aboutness of thought and talk in Chapter 5, and the sort of social-perspectival, dialogical inferential articulation that makes possible the objectivity of conceptual content in Chapter 6.

Chapter 2, "Action, Norms, and Practical Reasoning," extends the inferentialist paradigm in logic and semantics to encompass practical reasoning, culminating in noninferential discursive exit transitions in the form of intentional actions. Thus it combines an inferentialist approach to the contents of intentions with the inferentialist approach to the content of beliefs. It aims to do three things, corresponding to the three pieces of the title of the chapter:

> To explain in inferentialist terms the expressive role that distinguishes specifically *normative* vocabulary. That is, to say what it is the job of such vocabulary to make explicit. Doing this is saying what 'ought' means.
>
> To introduce a non-humean way of thinking about *practical reasoning*.
>
> To offer a broadly kantian account of the *will* as a rational faculty of practical reasoning.

The empiricist tradition seeks to trace back talk of reasons for action and norms governing action to underlying preferences and desires, which are understood both as intrinsically motivating and as the only sorts of things that can be intrinsically motivating. Thus any complete expression of a reason for action must include a specification of what it is that the agent wants, in virtue of which the reason functions (motivationally) as a reason for that agent. In the story told here, by contrast to this instrumentalist one, preferences and desires are explained in terms of commitments to certain patterns of practical inference, that is, in terms of what is a reason for what, instead of the other way around. Different sorts of normative vocabulary are presented as making it possible to codify, in the explicit form of claims (claimables), commitment to the propriety of different patterns of practical reasoning. Against this background, preferences and desires take their place as one sort of commitment among others, distinguished by its structure rather than by any privilege with respect either to reasons or to motivations for action.

Chapter 3, "Insights and Blindspots of Reliabilism," follows out the application of inferentialist semantic ideas to observation, that is, to perceptual noninferential discursive entrance transitions. The topic is the taking up into the conceptual order of the reliable differential responsive dispositions—for instance, to respond to red things by applying the concept *red*—that are essential to the contents of empirical concepts corresponding to observable states of affairs. The issue is approached through a discussion of contemporary epistemological reliabilism, which seeks to put appeals to reliable processes in place of more traditional appeals to inferential justifications—at least in epistemology, and perhaps also in understanding the contents of knowledge claims. Three insights and two blindspots of reliabilism are identified. What I call the *Founding Insight* points out that reliably formed true beliefs can qualify as knowledge even where the candidate knower cannot justify them. *Goldman's Insight* is that attributions of reliability must be relativized to reference classes. The *Implicit Insight* I discern in the examples used to motivate the first two claims is that attributions of reliability should be understood in terms of endorsements of a distinctive kind of *inference*. The *Conceptual Blindspot* results from overgeneralizing the founding insight from epistemology to semantics, taking it that because there can be knowledge even in cases where the knower cannot offer an inferential justification, it is therefore possible to understand the content of (knowledge) claims without appeal to inference at all. The *Naturalistic Blindspot* seeks in reliabilism the basis of a fully naturalized epistemology, one that need not appeal to norms or reasons at all. To avoid the Conceptual Blindspot, one must appreciate the significance of specifically inferential articulation in distinguishing representations that qualify as beliefs, and hence as candidates for knowledge. To avoid the Naturalistic Blindspot, one must appreciate that concern with reliability is concern with a distinctive kind of interpersonal inference. Appreciating the role of inference in these explanatory contexts is grasping the implicit insight of reliabilism. It is what is required to conserve and extend both the Founding Insight and Goldman's Insight. Thus, reliability should be understood in terms of the goodness of inference rather than the other way around.

The last three chapters take up the challenge of explaining the *referential* or *representational* dimension of concept use and conceptual content in terms of the *inferential* articulation that is here treated as primary in the order of explanation. To make a claim is to purport to state a fact. Chapter 4 offers an inferentialist account of what it is for the facts stated by true claimings to be about *objects,* and an inferentialist argument to the conclusion that facts *must* be about objects. An inferentialist pragmatism is committed to a top-down order of semantic explanation. It must give pride of place to *propositional* contents, for it is expressions with that sort of content that can play the basic inferential roles of premise and conclusion. The utterance of expressions that are suitable to appear in both these kinds of roles can have the pragmatic force or significance of *assertions,* and so the expressions in question can be identified as declarative *sentences.* Some further work is needed to distinguish and attribute conceptual content to *sub*sentential expressions such as singular terms and predicates, since they cannot serve as premises or conclusions in inferences. Frege's notion of *substitution* provides a way to extend the inferentialist account of the conceptual content of sentences to these sorts of subsentential expressions. It gives us a way of making sense of the notion of the contribution the occurrence of a subsentential expression makes to the correctness of inferences it appears in (as an element of a premise or conclusion). For we can notice which substitutions of subsentential expressions do, and which do not, preserve the correctness of inferences in which the sentences they occur in play the role of premise or conclusion. In that way, subsentential expressions can be accorded a substitutionally *indirect* inferential role.

Chapter 4, "What Are Singular Terms, and Why Are There Any?" falls into two parts, corresponding to the two parts of its title. The first argues that singular terms and predicates can be distinguished by the *structure* of the contributions they make to the correctness of substitution inferences involving sentences in which they occur. The second part argues that this is not a contingent or accidental structure. Very general conditions on inferential practice mandate that *if* inferentially significant subsentential structure is to be discerned in sentences at all, it *must* take the form of singular terms and predicates—that is, that if we are in the fact-stating line of work at all, the facts we state must be facts about objects and their properties and relations. Although in principle it is coherent to conceive of discursive practices that involve only sentential expressions devoid of internal structure, the expressive power of such languages is severely limited. For the productivity and creativity of language depend on the fact that an indefinite number of novel sentences can be produced and understood because they are constructed out of familiar subsentential elements. The central argument of the chapter is a derivation of the necessity of a singular term and predicate structure (in the precise substitution inferential sense specified in the first part of the chapter) from just two conditions: that there not be arbitrary restrictions on the carving up of sentences with a substitutional scalpel, and that the language contain the minimal expressive resources of *sentential* logic, namely, conditionals (or negation). Since, according to the inferentialist expressive view of logic, these are the locutions needed to make explicit within the language the material inferential relations in virtue of which ordinary nonlogical sentences have the conceptual contents they do, this means that singular terms and predicates will be substitutionally discernible within the basic sentences of any productive, projectible language capable of the minimal semantic self-consciousness made possible by the use of conditionals. The conclusion is that any language with sufficient expressive power concerning its own conceptual contents—never mind the character of the world it is being used to talk about—must take the form of sentences containing singular terms and predicates. That is, it must at least purport to state facts about objects and their properties and relations. I call this, rather grandly, *an expressive transcendental deduction of the necessity of objects.* It is certainly the most difficult part of the book, but the argument, though technical, requires no competence beyond familiarity with first-order logic.

At this point, then, we have seen in some sense what it is for our talk to be about *objects*. Chapter 5, "A Social Route from Reasoning to Representing," complements this discussion by offering a general account of *aboutness*. It pursues a double-barreled expressivist and pragmatist strategy. On the expressivist side, it aims to understand what is *implicit* in what one is *doing* in terms of the kind of *saying* that makes it *explicit*. Here the aim is to understand the activity of *representing* things as being thus-and-so in terms of the use of the explicitly representational locutions we use to express the representational dimension of concept use. If we put to one side technical, inevitably theory-laden philosophical terms such as 'denotes' and some uses of 'refers' and 'represents',[18] the claim is that the ordinary distinction between what we say or think and what we are talking of thinking *about* is expressed by using terms like 'of' and 'about'—not in phrases such as "the pen of my aunt" and "weighing about five pounds," but when used to express intentional directedness, as in "thinking of Benjamin Franklin" and "talking about wolves." These uses are in turn distinguished as those used to express *de re* attributions of propositional attitudes in the explicit, claimable form of ascriptions, such as "Adams claimed *of* Benjamin Franklin that he did not invent the lightning rod" (which might be paraphrased as "Adams represented Benjamin Franklin as not inventing the lightning rod"). In the pragmatist phase of the argument, then, we ask how one must *use* expressions in order for them to play the expressive role of explicit *de re* ascriptions of propositional attitude. The argument is completed by answering this question by an account of the *inferential* role distinctive of such ascriptions. The claim is that they codify certain *interpersonal* inferential commitments. The result is an account of the role of the explicitly representational vocabulary we use to express intentional directedness as codifying inferential commitments—that is, according to the expressive approach to logic, an account of its specifically *logical* expressive role.

Chapter 6, "Objectivity and the Normative Fine Structure of

Rationality," offers an argument in two parts, again corresponding to the two parts of the title. First is an argument for a thesis
about the norms governing any practices recognizable as including the giving of and asking for reasons—any practice in which
some performances have the implicit force or significance of
asserting and inferring—that is, according to the rationalist linguistic pragmatist line of thought pursued here, any genuinely *discursive* or concept-using practices. The claim is that those implicit
practical norms must, in order to count as discursive, come in at
least two flavors. It must be possible for some performances to
have the practical significance of undertaking *commitments.* For
asserting something is committing oneself to it, and the beliefs
those assertions express involve a kind of commitment. It is such
commitments that, in the first instance, stand in practical inferential relations—such as that *by* committing oneself overtly (assertionally) to Leo's being a lion, one thereby implicitly commits
oneself (whether one realizes it or not) to Leo's being a mammal.
And it is the contents of those commitments that stand in the
semantic inferential relations that can be made explicit by the use
of conditionals. But for such a structure of consequential commitment to count as involving assessments of *reasons,* there must be
in play also a notion of *entitlement* to one's commitments: the sort
of entitlement that is in question when we ask whether someone
has good *reasons* for her commitments. The question whether or
not one is committed to a certain claim(able) must be distinct
from the question whether or not one is entitled (by reasons) to
that commitment.

What I call here the 'normative fine structure of rationality' is
the constellation of kinds of broadly inferential relations that is
generated once we recognize these two sorts of normative status.
For now we can discern and distinguish at least three fundamental
ones: commitment-preserving inferences, entitlement-preserving
inferences, and incompatibilities. The first is a class of materially
good inferences (that is, ones whose correctness or incorrectness

essentially depends on or articulates the content of the nonlogical concepts that occur in their premises or conclusions) that generalizes what appears in the formalist tradition of logic as *deductive* inferences. The second is a class of materially good inferences that generalizes what appears in the formalist tradition as *inductive* inferences. The third has no classical analog. We can say that two claims are materially incompatible in case commitment to one precludes entitlement to the other. (This is a *normative* relation. One can undertake incompatible assertible commitments as easily and intelligibly as one can undertake incompatible practical ones, for instance, by making two promises both of which cannot be kept. What one cannot do is be *entitled* to both—indeed, in standard cases, to either—of the incompatible commitments.) This richer practical inferential structure provides important new resources for *logic*. For instance, one can define the *negation* of p as its minimum incompatible: it is the claim that is commitment entailed by every claim materially incompatible with p. It also provides important new resources for *semantics*. The final portion of the chapter shows how this structure of reasoning makes it possible to understand subjecting our claims to assessments according to a kind of correctness in which authority is invested in the *things* we are (in that central normative sense) talking *about* rather than in our *attitudes* toward them. Thus, by the end of the discussion we see how inferentially articulated conceptual norms can underwrite assessments of *objective* correctness of representation.

ONE

Semantic Inferentialism
and Logical Expressivism

I. Introduction

I want to introduce here a way of thinking about semantics that is different from more familiar ones, and on that basis also a new way of thinking about logic. In case that seems insufficiently ambitious, I will introduce these ideas by sketching a different way of thinking about some important episodes in the history of philosophy in the era that stretches from Descartes to Kant. I then explain and motivate the two ideas indicated in the title by putting together considerations drawn from three different thinkers, Frege, Dummett, and Sellars, or, as I think of them, the sage of Jena, the sage of Oxford, and the sage of Pittsburgh. In each case I pick up strands other than those usually emphasized when we read these figures.

II. Representationalism and Inferentialism

Pre-Kantian empiricists and rationalists alike were notoriously disposed to run together causal and conceptual issues, largely through insufficient appreciation of the normative character of the "order and connection of ideas" (Spinoza) that matters for concepts. But there is another, perhaps less appreciated, contrast in play during this period, besides that of the causal and the conceptual, the origin and the justification of our ideas. Enlightenment epistemology was always the home for two somewhat uneasily coexisting conceptions of the conceptual. The fundamental concept of the dominant and characteristic understanding of cognitive contentfulness in the period initiated by Descartes is of course *representation*. There is, however, a minority semantic tradition that takes *inference* rather than representation as its master concept.

Rationalists such as Spinoza and Leibniz accepted the central role of the concept of representation in explaining human cognitive activity. But they were not prepared to accept Descartes's strategy of treating the possession of representational content as an unexplained explainer—just dividing the world into what is by nature a representing and what by nature can only be represented. Each of them developed instead an account of what it is for one thing to represent another, in terms of the inferential significance of the representing. They were explicitly concerned, as Descartes was not, to be able to explain what it is for something to be understood, taken, treated, or employed *as* a representing *by* the subject: what it is for it to be a representing *to* or *for* that subject (to be "tanquam rem," as if of things, as Descartes puts it). Their idea was that the way in which representings point beyond themselves to something represented is to be understood in terms of *inferential* relations among representings. States and acts acquire content by being caught up in inferences, as premises and conclusions.

Thus a big divide within Enlightenment epistemology concerns the relative explanatory priority accorded to the concepts of representation and inference. The British empiricists were more puzzled than Descartes about representational purport: the property of so much as seeming to be *about* something. But they were clear in seeking to derive inferential relations from the contents of representings rather than the other way around. In this regard they belong to the still dominant tradition that reads inferential correctnesses off from representational correctnesses, which are assumed to be antecedently intelligible. That is why Hume could take for granted the contents of his individual representings but worry about how they could possibly underwrite the correctness of inductive inferences. The post-Cartesian rationalists, the claim goes, give rise to a tradition based on a complementary semantically reductive order of explanation. (So Kant, picking up the thread from this tradition, will come to see their involvement in counterfactually robust inferences as essential to empirical representations having the contents that they do.) These *inferentialists* seek to define representational properties in terms of inferential ones, which must accordingly be capable of being understood antecedently. They start with a notion of content as determining what is a *reason* for what, and understand truth and representation as features of ideas that are not only manifested in but actually *consist* in their role in reasoning. I actually think that the division of pre-Kantian philosophers into representationalists and inferentialists cuts according to deeper principles of their thought than does the nearly coextensional division of them into empiricists and rationalists, though it goes far beyond my brief to argue for that thesis here.

III. Inferentialism and Noninferential Reports

The concepts for which inferential notions of content are least obviously appropriate are those associated with observable properties, such as colors. For the characteristic use of such concepts is precisely in making *non*inferential reports, such as "This ball is red." One of the most important lessons we can learn from Sellars's masterwork, "Empiricism and the Philosophy of Mind" (as from the "Sense Certainty" section of Hegel's *Phenomenology*), is the inferentialist one that even such noninferential reports must be inferentially articulated. Without that requirement, we cannot tell the difference between noninferential reporters and automatic machinery such as thermostats and photocells, which also have reliable dispositions to respond differentially to stimuli. What is the important difference between a thermostat that turns the furnace on when the temperature drops to sixty degrees, or a parrot trained to say "That's red" in the presence of red things, on the one hand, and a genuine noninferential reporter of those circumstances, on the other? Each classifies particular stimuli as being of a general kind, the kind, namely, that elicits a repeatable response of a certain sort. In the same sense, of course, a chunk of iron classifies its environment as being of one of two kinds, depending on whether it responds by rusting or not. It is easy, but uninformative, to say that what distinguishes reporters from reliable responders is awareness. In this use the term is tied to the notion of understanding: the thermostat and the parrot do not understand their responses, those responses mean nothing to them, though they can mean something to us. We can add that the distinction wanted is that between merely responsive classification and specifically *conceptual* classification. The reporter must, as the parrot and thermostat do not, have the *concept* of temperature or cold. It is classifying under such a concept, something the reporter understands or grasps the meaning of, that makes the relevant difference.

It is at this point that Sellars introduces his central thought: that for a response to have *conceptual* content is just for it to play a role in the *inferential* game of making claims and giving and asking for reasons. To grasp or understand such a concept is to have practical mastery over the inferences it is involved in—to know, in the practical sense of being able to distinguish (a kind of know-*how*), what follows from the applicability of a concept, and what it follows from. The parrot does not treat "That's red" as incompatible with "That's green," nor as following from "That's scarlet" and entailing "That's colored." Insofar as the repeatable response is not, for the parrot, caught up in practical proprieties of inference and justification, and so of the making of further judgments, it is not a *conceptual* or a *cognitive* matter at all.

It follows immediately from such an inferential demarcation of the conceptual that in order to master *any* concepts, one must master *many* concepts. For grasp of one concept consists in mastery of at least some of its inferential relations to other concepts. Cognitively, grasp of just one concept is the sound of one hand clapping. Another consequence is that to be able to apply one concept *non*inferentially, one must be able to use others *inferentially*. For unless applying it can serve at least as a premise from which to draw inferential consequences, it is not functioning as a concept at all. So the idea that there could be an autonomous language game, one that could be played though one played no other, consisting entirely of noninferential reports (in the case Sellars is most concerned with in "Empiricism and the Philosophy of Mind," even of the current contents of one's own mind) is a radical mistake. (Of course this is compatible with there being languages without theoretical concepts, that is, concepts whose *only* use is inferential. The requirement is that for *any* concepts to have reporting uses, some concepts must have *non*reporting uses.)

IV. Frege on *Begriffliche Inhalt*

My purpose at the moment, however, is to pursue not the *consequences* of the inferential understanding of conceptual contents that Sellars recommends, but its *antecedents*. The predecessor it is most interesting to consider is the young Frege. Frege may seem an unlikely heir to this inferentialist tradition. After all, he is usually thought of as the father of the contemporary way of working out the *representationalist* order of explanation, which starts with an independent notion of relations of reference or denotation obtaining between mental or linguistic items and objects and sets of objects in the largely nonmental, nonlinguistic environment, and determines from these, in the familiar fashion, first truth conditions for the sentential representings built out of the subsentential ones, and then, from these, a notion of goodness of inference understood in terms of set-theoretic inclusions among the associated sets of truth conditions. But insofar as it is appropriate to read this twentieth-century story back into Frege at all, and I am not sure that it is, it would be possible only beginning with the Frege of the 1890s. He starts his semantic investigations not with the idea of reference but with that of inference. His seminal first work, the *Begriffsschrift* of 1879, takes as its aim the explication of "conceptual content" *(begriffliche Inhalt)*. The qualification "conceptual" is explicitly construed in inferential terms:

> There are two ways in which the content of two judgments may differ; it may, or it may not, be the case that all inferences that can be drawn from the first judgment when combined with certain other ones can always also be drawn from the second when combined with the same other judgments. The two propositions 'the Greeks defeated the Persians at Plataea' and 'the Persians were defeated by the Greeks at Plataea' differ in the former way; even if a slight difference of sense is discernible, the agreement in sense is preponderant. Now I call that part of the content that is the same in both the conceptual content. Only this has significance for our symbolic language [*Begriffsschrift*] . . . In my formalized language [*BGS*] . . . only that part of judgments which affects the possible inferences is taken into consideration. Whatever is needed for a correct [*richtig*, usually misleadingly translated as "valid"] inference is fully expressed; what is not needed is . . . not.[1]

Two claims have the same conceptual content if and only if they have the same inferential role: a good inference is never turned into a bad one by substituting one for the other. This way of specifying the explanatory target to which semantic theories, including referential ones, are directed is picked up by Frege's student Carnap, who in *The Logical Syntax of Language* defines the content of a sentence as the class of nonvalid sentences which are its consequences (that is, can be inferred from it). Sellars in turn picks up the idea from him, as his references to this definition indicate.

By contrast, the tradition Frege initiated in the 1890s makes truth, rather than inference, primary in the order of explanation. Dummett says of this shift:

> In this respect (and [Dummett implausibly but endearingly hastens to add] in this respect alone) Frege's new approach to logic was retrograde. He characterized logic by saying that, while all sciences have truth as their goal, in logic truth is not merely the goal, but the object of study. The traditional answer to the question what is the subject-matter of logic is, however, that it is, not truth, but inference, or, more properly, the relation of logical consequence. This was the received opinion all through the doldrums of logic, until the subject was revitalized by Frege; and it is, surely, the correct view.[2]

And again:

> It remains that the representation of logic as concerned with a characteristic of sentences, truth, rather than of transitions from sentences to sentences, had highly deleterious effects both in logic and in philosophy. In philosophy it led to a concentration on logical truth and its generalization, analytic truth, as the problematic notions, rather than on the notion of a statement's being a deductive consequence of other statements, and hence to solutions involving a distinction between two supposedly utterly different kinds of truth, analytic truth and contingent truth, which would have appeared preposterous and irrelevant if the central problem had from the start been taken to be that of the character of the relation of deductive consequence.[3]

The important thing to realize is that the young Frege has not yet made this false step. Two further points to keep in mind regarding this passage are, first, shifting from concern with inference to concern with truth is one move, understanding truth in terms of prior primitive reference relations is another. Since the mature Frege treats truth as indefinable and primitive, the extraction of a representationalist commitment even from the texts of the 1890s requires further showing (compare Davidson's truth-without-reference view in our own day). Second, understanding the topic of logic in terms of inference is not the same as seeing it in terms of logical inference, or of "deductive consequence," as Dummett puts it (I talk about this below under the heading of "formalism" about inference). The view propounded and attributed to Frege below is different from, and from the contemporary vantage point more surprising than, the one Dummett endorses here.

V. Material Inference

The kind of inference whose correctnesses determine the conceptual contents of its premises and conclusions may be called, following Sellars, *material* inferences. As examples, consider the inference from "Pittsburgh is to the west of Princeton" to "Princeton is to the east of Pittsburgh," and that from "Lightning is seen now" to "Thunder will be heard soon." It is the contents of the concepts *west* and *east* that make the first a good inference, and the contents of the concepts *lightning* and *thunder,* as well as the temporal concepts, that make the second appropriate. Endorsing these inferences is part of grasping or mastering those concepts, quite apart from any specifically *logical* competence.

Often, however, *inferential* articulation is identified with *logical* articulation. Material inferences are accordingly treated as a derivative category. The idea is that being rational—being subject to the normative force of the better reason, which so puzzled and fascinated the Greeks—can be understood as a purely logical capacity. In part this tendency was encouraged by merely verbally sloppy formulations of the crucial difference between the inferential force of reasons and the physically efficacious force of causes, which render it as the difference between 'logical' and 'natural' compulsion. Mistakes ensue, however, if the concept *logical* is employed with these circumstances of application conjoined with consequences of application that restrict the notion of logical force of reasons to formally valid inferences. The substantial commitment that is fundamental to this sort of approach is what Sellars calls "the received dogma . . . that the inference which finds its expression in 'It is raining, therefore the streets will be wet' is an enthymeme."[4]

According to this line of thought, wherever an inference is endorsed, it is because of belief in a conditional. Thus the instanced inference is understood as implicitly involving the conditional "If it is raining, then the streets will be wet." With that "suppressed" premise supplied, the inference is an instance of the formally valid scheme of conditional detachment. The "dogma" expresses a commitment to an order of explanation that treats all inferences as good or bad solely in virtue of their form, with the contents of the claims they involve mattering only for the truth of the (implicit) premises. According to this way of setting things out, there is no such thing as material inference. This view, which understands "good inference" to mean "formally valid inference," postulating implicit premises as needed, might be called a formalist approach to inference. It trades primitive goodnesses of inference for the truth of conditionals. Doing so is taking the retrograde step that Dummett complains about. (It is also what introduces the problem Lewis Carroll exposes in "Achilles and the Tortoise.") The grasp of logic that is attributed must be an implicit grasp, since it need be manifested only in distinguishing material inferences as good and bad, not in any further capacity to manipulate logical vocabulary or endorse tautologies involving them. But what then is the explanatory payoff from attributing such an implicit logical ability rather than just the capacity to assess proprieties of material inference?

The approach Sellars endorses is best understood by reference to the full list of alternatives he considers:

> We have been led to distinguish the following six conceptions of the status of material rules of inference:
>
> (1) Material rules are as essential to meaning (and hence to language and thought) as formal rules, contributing to the architectural detail of its structure within the flying buttresses of logical form.
>
> (2) While not essential to meaning, material rules of inference have an original authority not derived from formal rules, and play an indispensable role in our thinking on matters of fact.
>
> (3) Same as (2) save that the acknowledgment of material rules of inference is held to be a dispensable feature of thought, at best a matter of convenience.
>
> (4) Material rules of inference have a purely derivative authority, though they are genuinely rules of inference.
>
> (5) The sentences which raise these puzzles about material rules of inference are merely abridged formulations of logically valid inferences. (Clearly the distinction between an inference and the formulation of an inference would have to be explored.)
>
> (6) Trains of thought which are said to be governed by "material rules of inference" are actually not inferences at all, but rather activated associations which mimic inference, concealing their intellectual nudity with stolen "therefores."[5]

His own position is that an expression has conceptual content conferred on it by being caught up in, playing a certain role in, material inferences: "It is the first (or 'rationalistic') alternative to which we are committed. According to it, material transformation rules determine the descriptive meaning of the expressions of a language within the framework provided by its logical transformation rules . . . In traditional language, the 'content' of concepts as well as their logical 'form' is determined by the rules of the Understanding."[6]

Should inferentialist explanations begin with inferences pertaining to propositional *form* or those pertaining to propositional *content?* One important consideration is that the notion of formally valid inferences is definable in a natural way from that of materially correct ones, while there is no converse route. For given a subset of vocabulary that is privileged or distinguished somehow, an inference can be treated as good in virtue of its form, with respect to that vocabulary, just in case

It is a materially good inference, and

It cannot be turned into a materially bad one by substituting nonprivileged for nonprivileged vocabulary in its premises and conclusions.

Notice that this substitutional notion of formally good inferences need have nothing special to do with *logic*. If it is *logical* form that is of interest, then one must antecedently be able to distinguish some vocabulary as peculiarly logical. That done, the Fregean semantic strategy of looking for inferential features that are invariant under substitution yields a notion of *logically* valid inferences. But if one picks out *theo*logical (or aesthetic) vocabulary as privileged, then looking at which substitutions of nontheological (or nonaesthetic) vocabulary for nontheological (nonaesthetic) vocabulary preserve material goodness of inference will pick out inferences good in virtue of their *theo*logical (or aesthetic) form. According to this way of thinking, the *formal* goodness of inferences derives from and is explained in terms of the *material* goodness of inferences, and so ought not to be appealed to in explaining it. Frege's inferentialist way of specifying the characteristic linguistic role in virtue of which vocabulary qualifies as logical is discussed below.

VI. Elucidative Rationality

So far I have indicated briefly two related claims: that conceptual contents are inferential roles, and that the inferences that matter for such contents in general must be conceived to include those that are in some sense *materially correct,* not just those that are *formally valid.* I will argue in a moment that a commitment to the second of these, no less than the first, is to be found already in Frege's early writings, though not in the developed form to which Sellars brings it. But in both thinkers these ideas are combined with a third, which I believe makes this line of thought especially attractive. In one of his early papers, Sellars introduces the idea this way: "Socratic method serves the purpose of making explicit the rules we have adopted for thought and action, and I shall be interpreting our judgments to the effect that A causally necessitates B as the expression of a rule governing our use of the terms 'A' and 'B'."[7] Sellars understands such modal statements as inference licenses, which formulate as the content of a claim the appropriateness of inferential transitions. More than this, he understands the function of such statements to be making explicit, in the form of assertible rules, commitments that had hitherto remained implicit in inferential practices. Socratic method is a way of bringing our practices under rational control by expressing them explicitly in a form in which they can be confronted with objections and alternatives, a form in which they can be exhibited as the conclusions of inferences seeking to justify them on the basis of premises advanced as reasons, and as premises in further inferences exploring the consequences of accepting them.

In the passage just quoted, Sellars tells us that the enterprise within which we ought to understand the characteristic function of inference licenses is a form of rationality that centers on the notion of *expression:* making *explicit* in a form that can be thought or said what is *implicit* in what is done. This is a dark and pregnant claim, but I believe it epitomizes a radical and distinctive insight.

In what follows I hope to shed some light on it and its role in an inferentialist vision of things. The general idea is that the paradigmatically rational process that Sellars invokes under the heading of "Socratic method" depends on the possibility of making implicit commitments explicit in the form of claims. *Expressing* them in this sense is bringing them into the game of giving and asking for reasons as playing the special sort of role in virtue of which something has a conceptual content at all, namely, an inferential role, as premise and conclusion of inferences. This sort of rationality is distinct from, but obviously related to, the sort of rationality that then consists in making the appropriate inferential moves. Even totalitarian versions of the latter—for instance, those that would assimilate all goodness of inference to logical validity, or to instrumental prudence (that is, efficiency at getting what one wants)—depend on the possibility of expressing considerations in a form in which they can be given as reasons, and reasons demanded for them. All the more does Socratic reflection on our practices—particularly on those material-inferential practices that determine the conceptual contents of thoughts and beliefs—depend on the possibility of their explicit expression.

VII. Frege on the Expressive Role of Logic

To begin to explicate this notion of explication, it is helpful to return to the consideration of the young Frege's inferentialist program. Frege's *Begriffsschrift* is remarkable not only for the inferential idiom in which it specifies its topic, but equally for how it conceives its relation to that topic. The task of the work is officially an expressive one: not to prove something but to say something. Frege's logical notation is designed for expressing conceptual contents, making explicit the inferential involvements that are implicit in anything that possesses such content. As the passage quoted earlier puts it, "Whatever is needed for a correct inference is fully expressed." Talking about this project, Frege says: "Right from the start I had in mind the expression of a content. . . But the content is to be rendered more exactly than is done by verbal language. . . Speech often only indicates by inessential marks or by imagery what a concept-script should spell out in full."[8] The concept-script is a formal language for the explicit codification of conceptual contents. In the Preface to *Begriffsschrift*, Frege laments that even in science concepts are formed haphazardly, so that the ones employing them are scarcely aware of what they mean, of what their content really is. When the correctness of particular inferences is at issue, this sort of unclarity may preclude rational settlement of the issue. What is needed is a notation within which the rough-and-ready conceptual contents of the sciences, beginning with mathematics, can be reformulated so as to wear their contents on their sleeves. The explanatory target here avowedly concerns a sort of inference, not a sort of truth, and the sort of inference involved is content-conferring material inferences, not the derivative formal ones.

Frege explicitly contrasts his approach with that of those, such as Boole, who conceive their formal language only in terms of formal inference, and so express no material contents:

> The reason for this inability to form concepts in a scientific manner lies in the lack of one of the two components of which every highly developed language must consist. That is, we may distinguish the formal part . . . from the material part proper. The signs of arithmetic correspond to the latter. What we still lack is the logical cement that will bind these building stones firmly together. . . In contrast, Boole's symbolic logic only represents the formal part of the language.[9]

By contrast, Frege continues:

1. My concept-script has a more far-reaching aim than Boolean logic, in that it strives to make it possible to present a content when combined with arithmetical and geometrical signs . . .

2. Disregarding content, within the domain of pure logic it also, thanks to the notation for generality, commands a somewhat wider domain . . .

4. It is in a position to represent the formation of the concepts actually needed in science . . .[10]

It is the wider domain to which his expressive ambition extends that Frege sees as characteristic of his approach. Since contents are determined by inferences, expressing inferences explicitly will permit the expression of any sort of content at all: "It seems to me to be easier still to extend the domain of this formula language to include geometry. We would only have to add a few signs for the intuitive relations that occur there. . . The transition to the pure theory of motion and then to mechanics and physics could follow at this point."[11]

Frege's early understanding of logic offers some specific content to the notion of explicitly expressing what is implicit in a conceptual content, which is what is required to fill in a notion of expressive or elucidating rationality that might be laid alongside (and perhaps even be discovered to be presupposed by) notions of rationality as accurate representation, as logically valid inference, and as instrumental practical reasoning. Before one takes the fateful step from seeing logic as an attempt to codify inferences to seeing it as the search for a special kind of truth, which Dummett bemoans, Frege's aim is to introduce vocabulary that will let one *say* (explicitly) what otherwise one can only *do* (implicitly). Consider the conditional, with which the *Begriffsschrift* begins. Frege says of it: "The precisely defined hypothetical relation between contents of possible judgments [Frege's conditional] has a similar significance for the foundation of my concept-script to that which identity of extensions has for Boolean logic."[12] I think it is hard to overestimate the importance of this passage in understanding what is distinctive about Frege's *Begriffsschrift* project. After all, contemporary Tarskian model-theoretic semantics depends precisely on relations among extensions. Frege is saying that his distinctive idea—in what is, after all, the founding document of modern formal logic—is to do things otherwise.

Why the conditional? Prior to the introduction of such a conditional locution, one could *do* something, one could treat a judgment as having a certain content (implicitly attribute that content to it) by endorsing various inferences involving it and rejecting others. After conditional locutions have been introduced, one can *say,* as part of the content of a claim (something that can serve as a premise and conclusion in inference), *that* a certain inference is acceptable. One is able to make explicit material inferential relations between an antecedent or premise and a consequent or conclusion. Since, according to the inferentialist view of conceptual contents, it is these implicitly recognized material inferential relations that conceptual contents consist in, the conditional permits such contents to be explicitly expressed. If there is a disagreement about the goodness of an inference, it is possible to say what the dispute is about and offer reasons one way or the other. The conditional is the paradigm of a locution that permits one to make inferential commitments explicit as the contents of judgments. In a similar fashion, introducing negation makes it possible to express explicitly material incompatibilities of sentences, which also contribute to their content. The picture is accordingly one whereby, first, formal validity of inferences is defined in terms of materially correct inferences and some privileged vocabulary; second, that privileged vocabulary is identified as logical vocabulary; and third, what it is for something to be a bit of logical vocabulary is explained in terms of its semantically expressive role.

Frege is not as explicit about the role of materially correct inferences as Sellars is, but his commitment to the notion is clear from the relation between two of the views that have been extracted from the *Begriffsschrift:* expressivism about logic and inferentialism about content. Expressivism about logic means that Frege treats logical vocabulary as having a distinctive expressive role:

making explicit the inferences that are implicit in the conceptual contents of nonlogical concepts. Inferentialism about those conceptual contents means taking them to be identified and individuated by their inferential roles. Together these views require that it be coherent to talk about inference prior to the introduction of specifically logical vocabulary, and so prior to the identification of any inferences as good in virtue of their form. In the context of an inferential understanding of conceptual contents, an expressivist approach presupposes a notion of nonlogical inference, the inferences in virtue of which concepts have nonlogical content. Thus the young Frege envisages a field of material inferences that confer conceptual content on sentences caught up in them. So although Frege does not offer an explanation of the concept, in the *Begriffsschrift* his expressive, explicitating project commits him to something playing the role Sellars later picks out by the phrase "material inference."

VIII. Dummett's Model and Gentzen

So far three themes have been introduced:

That conceptual content is to be understood in terms of role in reasoning rather than exclusively in terms of representation;

That the capacity for such reasoning is not to be identified exclusively with mastery of a logical calculus; and

That besides theoretical and practical reasoning using contents constituted by their role in material inferences, there is a kind of expressive rationality that consists in making implicit content-conferring inferential commitments explicit as the contents of assertible commitments. In this way, the material inferential practices, which govern and make possible the game of giving and asking for reasons, are brought into that game, and so into consciousness, as explicit topics of discussion and justification.

These three themes, to be found in the early works of both Frege and Sellars, provide the beginnings of the structure within which modern inferentialism develops. These ideas can be made more definite by considering a general model of conceptual contents as inferential roles that has been recommended by Dummett. According to that model, the use of any linguistic expression or concept has two aspects: the *circumstances* under which it is correctly applied, uttered, or used, and the appropriate *consequences* of its application, utterance, or use. Though Dummett does not make this point, this model can be connected to inferentialism via the principle that the content to which one is committed by using the concept or expression may be represented by the inference one implicitly endorses by such use, the inference, namely, from the circumstances of appropriate employment to the appropriate consequences of such employment.

The original source for the model lies in a treatment of the grammatical category of sentential connectives. Dummett's two-aspect model is a generalization of a standard way of specifying the inferential roles of logical connectives, owing ultimately to Gentzen. Gentzen famously defined connectives by specifying introduction rules, or inferentially sufficient conditions for the employment of the connective, and elimination rules, or inferentially necessary consequences of the employment of the connective. So, to define the inferential role of an expression '&' of Boolean conjunction, one specifies that anyone who is committed to p, and committed to q, is thereby to count also as committed to $p\&q$, and that anyone who is committed to $p\&q$ is thereby committed both to p and to q. The first schema specifies, by means of expressions that do not contain the connective, the circumstances under which one is committed to claims expressed by sentences that do contain (as principal connective) the connective whose inferential role is being defined, that is, the sets of premises that entail them. The second schema specifies, by means of expressions that do not contain the connective, the consequences of being committed to claims expressed by sentences that do contain (as principal connective) the connective whose inferential role is being defined, that is, the sets of consequences that they entail.

IX. Circumstances and Consequences for Sentences

Dummett makes a remarkable contribution to inferentialist approaches to conceptual content by showing how this model can be generalized from logical connectives to provide a uniform treatment of the meanings of expressions of other grammatical categories, in particular sentences, predicates and common nouns, and singular terms. The application to the propositional contents expressed by whole sentences is straightforward. What corresponds to an *introduction* rule for a propositional content is the set of *sufficient* conditions for asserting it, and what corresponds to an *elimination* rule is the set of *necessary* consequences of asserting it, that is, what follows from doing so. Dummett says: "Learning to use a statement of a given form involves, then, learning two things: the conditions under which one is justified in making the statement; and what constitutes acceptance of it, i.e., the consequences of accepting it."[13] Dummett presents his model as specifying two fundamental features of the *use* of linguistic expressions, an idea I will return to below. In what follows here, though, I apply it in the context of the previous ideas to bring into relief the implicit material inferential *content* a concept or expression acquires in virtue of being used in the ways specified by these two 'aspects'. The link between pragmatic significance and inferential content is supplied by the fact that asserting a sentence is implicitly undertaking a commitment to the correctness of the material inference from its circumstances to its consequences of application.

Understanding or grasping a propositional content is here presented not as the turning on of a Cartesian light, but as practical mastery of a certain kind of inferentially articulated doing: responding differentially according to the circumstances of proper application of a concept, and distinguishing the proper inferential consequences of such application. This is not an all-or-none affair; the metallurgist understands the concept *tellurium* better than I do, for training has made her master of the inferential intricacies of its employment in a way that I can only crudely approximate. Thinking clearly is on this inferentialist rendering a matter of knowing what one is committing oneself to by a certain claim, and what would entitle one to that commitment. Writing clearly is providing enough clues for a reader to infer what one intends to be committed to by each claim, and what one takes it would entitle one to that commitment. Failure to grasp either of these components is failure to grasp the inferential commitment that use of the concept involves, and so failure to grasp its conceptual content.

Failure to think about both the circumstances and consequences of application leads to semantic theories that are literally one-sided. Verificationists, assertibilists, and reliabilists make the mistake of treating the *first* aspect as exhausting content. Understanding or grasping a content is taken to consist in practically mastering the circumstances under which one becomes entitled or committed to endorse a claim, quite apart from any grasp of what one becomes entitled or committed to by such endorsement. But this cannot be right. For claims can have the same circumstances of application and different consequences of application, as for instance "I foresee that I will write a book about Hegel" and "I will write a book about Hegel" do. We can at least regiment a use of 'foresee' that makes the former sentence have just the same assertibility conditions as the latter. But substituting the one for the other turns the very safe conditional "If I will write a book about Hegel, then I will write a book about Hegel," into the risky "If I *foresee* that I will write a book about Hegel, then I will write a book about Hegel." The possibility that I might be hit by a bus does not affect the assessment of the inference codified by the first conditional, but is quite relevant to the assessment of the second inference.

And the point of the discussion, at the beginning of this chapter, of Sellars's application of inferentialist ideas to the understanding of noninferential reports was that parrots and photocells and so on might reliably discriminate the circumstances in which the concept *red* should be applied, without thereby grasping that concept, precisely in the case where they have no mastery of the consequences of such application—when they cannot tell that it follows from something being red that it is colored, that it is not a prime number, and so on. You do not convey to me the content of the concept *gleeb* by supplying me with an infallible gleebness tester which lights up when and only when exposed to gleeb things. I would in that case know what things were gleeb without knowing what I was saying about them when I called them that, what I had found out about them or committed myself to. Dummett offers two examples of philosophically important concepts where it is useful to be reminded of this point:

> An account, however accurate, of the conditions under which some predicate is rightly applied may thus miss important intuitive features of its meaning; in particular, it may leave out what we take to be the point of our use of the predicate. A philosophical account of the notion of truth can thus not necessarily be attained by a definition of the predicate 'true', even if one is possible, since such a definition may be correct only in the sense that it specifies correctly the application of the predicate, while leaving the connections between this predicate and other notions quite obscure.[14]

Even more clearly:

> A good example would be the word 'valid' as applied to various forms of argument. We might reckon the syntactic characterization of validity as giving the criterion for applying the predicate 'valid' to an argument, and the semantic characterization of validity as giving the consequences of such an application . . . [I]f

[one] is taught in a very unimaginative way, [one] may see the classification of arguments into valid and invalid ones as resembling the classification of poems into sonnets and non-sonnets, and so fail to grasp that the fact that an argument is valid provides any grounds for accepting the conclusion if one accepts the premises. We should naturally say that [one] had missed the point of the distinction.[15]

Pragmatists of the classical sort, by contrast, make the converse mistake of identifying propositional contents exclusively with the *consequences* of endorsing a claim, looking downstream to the claim's role as a premise in practical reasoning and ignoring its proper antecedents upstream. (For present purposes, that the emphasis is on *practical* consequences does not matter.) Yet one can know what follows from the claim that someone is responsible for a particular action, that an action is immoral or sinful, that a remark is true or in bad taste, without for that reason counting as understanding the claims involved, if one has no idea when it is appropriate to make those claims or apply those concepts. Being classified as AWOL does have the consequence that one is liable to be arrested, but the specific circumstances under which one acquires that liability are equally essential to the concept.

X. 'Derivation', Prior, Belnap, and Conservativeness

Of course, such one-sided theories do not simply ignore the aspects of content they do not treat as central. Dummett writes:

> Most philosophical observations about meaning embody a claim to perceive . . . a simple pattern: the meaning of a sentence consists in the conditions for its truth and falsity, or in the method of its verification, or in the practical consequences of accepting it. Such dicta cannot be taken to be so naive as to involve overlooking the fact that there are many other features of the use of a sentence than the one singled out as being that in which its meaning

consists: rather, the hope is that we shall be able to give an account of the connection that exists between the different aspects of meaning. One particular aspect will be taken as central, as constitutive of the meaning of any given sentence . . . ; all other features of the use of the sentence will then be explained by a uniform account of their derivation from that feature taken as central.[16]

I think this is a very helpful way to think about the structure of theories of meaning in general, but two observations should be made. First, the principle that the task of a theory of meaning is to explain the use of expressions to which meanings are attributed does not mandate identifying meaning with an aspect of use. Perhaps meanings are to use as theoretical entities are to the observable ones whose antics they are postulated to explain. We need not follow Dummett in his semantic instrumentalism. Second, one might deny that there are meanings in this sense, that is, deny that all the features of the use of an expression can be derived in a uniform way from anything we know about it. Dummett suggests that this is the view of the later Wittgenstein. One who takes language to be a motley in this sense will deny that there are such things as meanings to be the objects of a theory (without, of course, denying that expressions are meaningful). Keeping these caveats in mind, we will find that pursuing this notion of *derivation* provides a helpful perspective on the idea of conceptual contents articulated according to material inferences, and on the role of explicit inference licenses such as conditional statements in expressing and elucidating such inferences, and so such contents.

For the special case of defining the inferential roles of logical connectives by pairs of sets of rules for their introduction and for their elimination, which motivates Dummett's broader model, there is a special condition which it is appropriate to impose on the relation between the two sorts of rules: "In the case of a logical constant, we may regard the introduction rules governing it as giving conditions for the assertion of a statement of which it is the main operator, and the elimination rules as giving the consequences of such a statement: the demand for harmony between them is then expressible as the requirement that the addition of the constant to a language produces a conservative extension of that language."[17] Recognition of the appropriateness of such a requirement arises from consideration of connectives with 'inconsistent' contents. As Prior[18] pointed out, if we define a connective, which after Belnap we may call "tonk,"[19] as having the introduction rule proper to disjunction and the elimination rule proper to conjunction, then the first rule licenses the transition from p to p tonk q, for arbitrary q, and the second licenses the transition from p tonk q to q, and we have what he called a "runabout inference ticket" permitting any arbitrary inference. Prior thought that this possibility shows the bankruptcy of Gentzen-style definitions of inferential roles. Belnap shows rather that when logical vocabulary is being introduced, one must constrain such definitions by the condition that the rule not license any inferences involving only old vocabulary that were not already licensed before the logical vocabulary was introduced, that is, that the new rules provide an inferentially conservative extension of the original field of inferences. Such a constraint is necessary and sufficient to keep from getting into trouble with Gentzen-style definitions. But the expressive account of what disinguishes logical vocabulary shows us a deep *reason* for this demand; it is needed not only to avoid horrible consequences but also because otherwise logical vocabulary cannot perform its expressive function. Unless the introduction and elimination rules are inferentially conservative, the introduction of the new vocabulary licenses new material inferences, and so alters the contents associated with the old vocabulary. So if logical vocabulary is to play its distinctive expressive role of making explicit the original material inferences, and so conceptual contents expressed by the old vocabulary, it must be a criterion of adequacy for introducing logical vocabulary that no new inferences involving only the old vocabulary be made appropriate thereby.

XI. 'Boche' and the Elucidation of Inferential Commitments

The problem of what Dummett calls a lack of "harmony" between the circumstances and the consequences of application of a concept may arise for concepts with material contents, however. Seeing how it does provides further help in understanding the notion of expressive rationality, and the way in which the explicitating role of logical vocabulary contributes to the clarification of concepts. For conceptual change can be

> motivated by the desire to attain or preserve a harmony between the two aspects of an expression's meaning. A simple case would be that of a pejorative term, e.g. 'Boche'. The conditions for applying the term to someone is that he is of German nationality; the consequences of its application are that he is barbarous and more prone to cruelty than other Europeans. We should envisage the connections in both directions as sufficiently tight as to be involved in the very meaning of the word: neither could be severed without altering its meaning. Someone who rejects the word does so because he does not want to permit a transition from the grounds for applying the term to the consequences of doing so. The addition of the term 'Boche' to a language which did not previously contain it would produce a non-conservative extension, i.e. one in which certain other statements which did not contain the term were inferable from other statements not containing it which were not previously inferable.[20]

This crucial passage makes a number of points that are worth untangling. First of all, it shows how concepts can be criticized on the basis of substantive beliefs. If one does not believe that the inference from German nationality to cruelty is a good one, one must eschew the concept or expression 'Boche'. For one cannot deny that there are any Boche—that is just denying that anyone is German, which is patently false. One cannot admit that there are Boche and deny that they are cruel—that is just attempting to take back with one claim what one has committed oneself to with another. One can only refuse to employ the concept, on the grounds that it embodies an inference one does not endorse.

I have been told (by Jonathan Bennett) that the prosecutor at Oscar Wilde's trial at one point read out some of the more hair-raising passages from *The Importance of Being Earnest* and said, "I put it to you, Mr. Wilde, that this is *blasphemy*. Is it or is it not?" Wilde made exactly the reply he ought to make—indeed, the only one he could make—given the considerations being presented here and the circumstances and consequences of application of the concept in question. He said, "Sir, 'blasphemy' is not one of my words."

Highly charged words such as 'nigger', 'whore', 'faggot', 'lady', 'Communist', 'Republican' have seemed to some a special case because they couple 'descriptive' circumstances of application to 'evaluative' consequences. But this is not the only sort of expression embodying inferences that requires close scrutiny. The use of any concept or expression involves commitment to an inference from its grounds to its consequences of application. Critical thinkers, or merely fastidious ones, must examine their idioms to be sure that they are prepared to endorse and so defend the appropriateness of the material inferential transitions implicit in the concepts they employ. In Reason's fight against thought debased by prejudice and propaganda, the first rule is that potentially controversial material inferential commitments should be made explicit as claims, exposing them both as vulnerable to reasoned challenge and as in need of reasoned defense. They must not be allowed to remain curled up inside loaded phrases such as 'enemy of the people' or 'law and order'.

It is in this process that formal logical vocabulary such as the conditional plays its explicitating role. It permits the formulation, as explicit claims, of the inferential commitments that otherwise remain implicit and unexamined in the contents of material concepts. Logical locutions make it possible to display the relevant grounds and consequences and to assert their inferential relation. Formulating as an explicit claim the inferential commitment implicit in the content brings it out into the open as liable to challenges and demands for justification, just as with any assertion. In this way explicit expression plays an elucidating role, functioning to groom and improve our inferential commitments, and so our conceptual contents—a role, in short, in the practices of reflective rationality or 'Socratic method'.

But if Dummett is suggesting that what is wrong with the concept *Boche* (or *nigger*) is that its addition represents a nonconservative extension of the rest of the language, he is mistaken. Its nonconservativeness just shows that it has a substantive content, in that it implicitly involves a material inference that is not already implicit in the contents of other concepts being employed. Outside of logic, this is no bad thing. Conceptual progress in science often consists in introducing just such novel contents. The concept of temperature was introduced with certain criteria or circumstances of appropriate application, and certain consequences of application. As new ways of measuring temperature are introduced, and new theoretical and practical consequences of temperature measurements adopted, the complex inferential commitment that determines the significance of using the concept of temperature evolves.

The proper question to ask in evaluating the introduction and evolution of a concept is not whether the inference embodied is one that is already endorsed, so that no new content is really involved, but rather whether that inference is one that *ought* to be endorsed. The problem with 'Boche' or 'nigger' is not that once we explicitly confront the material inferential commitment that gives the term its content it turns out to be novel, but that it can then be seen to be indefensible and inappropriate—a commitment we cannot become entitled to. We want to be aware of the inferential commitments our concepts involve, to be able to make them explicit, and to be able to justify them. But there are other ways of justifying them than showing that we were already implicitly committed to them before introducing or altering the concept in question.

XII. Harmony and Material Inference

Even in the cases where it does make sense to identify harmony of circumstances and consequences with inferential conservativeness, the attribution of conservativeness is always relative to a background set of material inferential practices, the ones that are conservatively extended by the vocabulary in question. Conservativeness is a property of the conceptual content only in the context of other contents, not something it has by itself. Thus there can be pairs of logical connectives, either of which is all right by itself, but both of which cannot be included in a consistent system. It is a peculiar ideal of harmony that would be realized by a system of conceptual contents such that the material inferences implicit in every subset of concepts represented a conservative extension of the remaining concepts, in that no inferences involving only the remaining ones are licensed that are not licensed already by the contents associated just with those remaining concepts. Such a system is an idealization, because all of its concepts would already be out in the open; none remaining hidden, to be revealed only by drawing conclusions from premises that have never been conjoined before, following out unexplored lines of reasoning, drawing consequences one was not previously aware one would be entitled or committed to by some set of premises. In short, this would be a case where Socratic reflection, making implicit commitments explicit and examining their consequences and possible justifications, would never motivate one to alter contents or commitments. Such complete transparency of commitment and entitlement is in some sense an ideal projected by the sort of Socratic practice that finds current contents and commitments wanting by confronting them with one another, pointing out inferential features of each of which we were unaware. But as Wittgenstein teaches in general, it should not be assumed that our scheme is like this, or depends on an underlying set of contents like this, just because we are obliged to remove any particular ways in which we discover it to fall short.

These are reasons to part company with the suggestion, forwarded in the passage above, that inferential conservatism is a necessary condition of a 'harmonious' concept—one that will not 'tonk up' a conceptual scheme. In a footnote, Dummett explicitly denies that conservativeness can in general be treated as a sufficient condition of harmony: "This is not to say that the character of the harmony demanded is always easy to explain, or that it can always be accounted for in terms of the notion of a conservative extension . . . [T]he most difficult case is probably the vexed problem of personal identity."[21] In another place, this remark about personal identity is laid out in more detail:

> We have reasonably sharp criteria which we apply in ordinary cases for deciding questions of personal identity: and there are also fairly clear consequences attaching to the settlement of such a question one way or the other, namely those relating to ascriptions of responsibility, both moral and legal, to the rights and obligations which a person has . . . What is much harder is to give an account of the connection between the criteria for the truth of a statement of personal identity and the consequences of accepting it. We can easily imagine people who use different criteria from ours . . . Precisely what would make the criteria they used criteria for personal identity would lie in their attaching the same consequence, in regard to responsibility, motivation, etc., to their statements of personal identity as we do to ours. If there

existed a clear method for deriving, as it were, the consequences of a statement from the criteria for its truth, then the difference between such people and ourselves would have the character of a factual disagreement, and one side would be able to show the other to be wrong. If there were no connection between truth-grounds and consequences, then the disagreement between us would lie merely in a preference for different concepts, and there would be no right or wrong in the matter at all.[22]

Dummett thinks that there is a general problem concerning the way in which the circumstances and consequences of application of expressions or concepts ought to fit together. Some sort of 'harmony' seems to be required between these two aspects of the use. The puzzling thing, he seems to be saying, is that the harmony required cannot happily be assimilated either to compulsion by facts or to the dictates of freely chosen meanings. But the options—matter of fact or relation of ideas, expression of commitment as belief or expression of commitment as meaning—are not ones that readers of "Two Dogmas of Empiricism" ought to be tempted to treat as exhaustive.

The notion of a completely factual issue that Dummett appeals to in this passage is one in which the applicability of a concept is settled straightforwardly by the application of other concepts—the concepts that specify the necessary and sufficient conditions that determine the truth conditions of claims involving the original concept. This conception, envisaged by a model of conceptual content as necessary and sufficient conditions, seems to require a conceptual scheme that is ideally transparent in the way mentioned above, in that it is immune to Socratic criticism. For that conception insists that these coincide in that the jointly sufficient conditions already entail the individually necessary ones, so that it is attractive to talk about content as truth conditions rather than focusing on the substantive inferential commitments that relate the sufficient to the distinct necessary conditions, as recommended here. By contrast to this either/or, in a picture according to which conceptual contents are conferred on expressions by their being caught up in a structure of inferentially articulated commitments and entitlements, material inferential commitments are a necessary part of any package of practices that includes material doxastic commitments.

The circumstances and consequences of application of a nonlogical concept may stand in a substantive material inferential relation. To ask what sort of 'harmony' they should exhibit is to ask what material inferences we ought to endorse, and so what conceptual contents we ought to employ. This is not the sort of question to which we ought to expect or welcome a general or wholesale answer. Grooming our concepts and material inferential commitments in the light of our assertional commitments, including those we find ourselves with noninferentially through observation, and the latter in the light of the former, is a messy, retail business.

Dummett thinks that a theory of meaning should take the form of an account of the nature of the 'harmony' that ought to obtain between the circumstances and the consequences of application of the concepts we ought to employ. If we shift our concern up a level now, to apply these considerations about the relations of circumstances to consequences of application to the contents of the concepts employed in the metalanguage in which we couch a semantic theory, the important point would be that we should not expect a theory of that sort to take the form of a specification of necessary and sufficient conditions for the circumstances and consequences of application of a concept to be harmonious. For that presupposes that the circumstances and consequences of application of the concept of *harmony* do not themselves stand in a substantive material inferential relation. On the contrary, insofar as the idea of a theory of semantic or inferential harmony makes sense at all, it must take the form of an investigation of the ongoing elucidative process, of the 'Socratic method' of discovering and repairing discordant concepts, which alone gives the notion of harmony any content. It is given content only by the process of harmonizing commitments, from which it is abstracted. In Sellars's characterization of expressive rationality, modal claims are assigned the expressive role of inference licenses, which make explicit a commitment that is implicit in the use of conceptual contents antecedently in play. Rules of this sort assert an authority over future practice, and answer for their entitlement both to the prior practice being codified and to concomitant inferential and doxastic commitments. In this way they may be likened to the principles formulated by judges at common law, intended both to codify prior practice, as represented by precedent, expressing explicitly as a rule what was implicit therein, and to have regulative authority for subsequent practice. The expressive task of making material inferential commitments explicit plays an essential role in the reflectively rational Socratic practice of harmonizing our commitments. For a commitment to become explicit is for it to be thrown into the game of giving and asking for reasons as something whose justification, in terms of other commitments and entitlements, is liable to question. Any theory of the sort of inferential harmony of commitments we are aiming at by engaging in this reflective, rational process must derive its credentials from its expressive adequacy to that practice before it should be accorded any authority over it.

XIII. From Semantics to Pragmatics

In the first part of this chapter I introduced three related ideas:

> the *inferential* understanding of conceptual content;
> the idea of *materially* good inferences; and
> the idea of *expressive* rationality.

These contrast, respectively, with

> an understanding of content exclusively according to the model
> of the *representation* of states of affairs (I think I have man-

aged to say rather a lot about conceptual content in this essay, without talking at all about what is represented by such contents);

an understanding of the goodness of inference exclusively on the model of *formal* validity; and

an understanding of rationality exclusively on the model of *instrumental* or means-end reasoning.

In the second part of the chapter these ideas were considered in relation to the representation of inferential role suggested by Dummett, in terms of the circumstances of appropriate application of an expression or concept and the appropriate consequences of such application. It is in the context of these ideas that I have sought to present an *expressive* view of the role of logic and its relation to the practices constitutive of rationality. That view holds out the hope of recovering for the study of *logic* a direct significance for projects that have been at the core of *philosophy* since its Socratic inception.

TWO

◆ ◆ ◆

Action, Norms, and Practical Reasoning

I. Some Background

In this chapter I aim to do three things, corresponding to the three elements of my title:

To explain the expressive role that distinguishes specifically *normative* vocabulary. That is, to say what it is the job of such vocabulary to make explicit. Doing this is saying what 'ought' means.

To introduce a non-Humean way of thinking about *practical reasoning*.

To offer a broadly Kantian account of the *will* as a rational faculty of practical reasoning.

The idea is to do that by exploiting the structural analogies between discursive exit transitions in action and discursive entry transitions in perception to show how the rational will can be understood as no more philosophically mysterious than our capacity to notice red things.

Practical reasoning often leads to action, so it is clear that there is an intimate connection between these two elements of my title. But one might wonder: why action and *norms*? Let me start with some background. The beginning of wisdom in thinking about these matters (as for so many others) is to look to Kant: the great, gray mother of us all. For we are in the privileged position of being downstream from the fundamental conceptual sea change effected by the replacement of concern with Cartesian certainty by concern with Kantian necessity—that is, of concern with our grip on concepts (Is it clear? Is it distinct?) by concern with their grip on us (Is this rule binding on us? Is it applicable to this case?). Kant's big idea is that what distinguishes judgment and action from the responses of merely natural creatures is neither their relation to some special stuff nor their peculiar transparency, but rather that they are what we are in a distinctive way *responsible* for. They express *commitments* of ours: commitments that we are answerable for in the sense that our *entitlement* to them is always potentially at issue; commitments that are *rational* in the sense that vindicating the corresponding entitlements is a matter of offering *reasons* for them.

Another big idea of Kant's—seeing the *judgment* as the smallest unit of experience—is a consequence of the first one. The logic he inherited started with a doctrine of *terms,* divided into the singular and the general, proceeded to a doctrine of *judgment* (understood in terms of predicating a general term of a singular one), and thence to a doctrine of *consequences* or inferences. Kant starts with judgment because that is the smallest unit for which we can be *responsible.* (This thought is taken over by Frege, who begins with the units to which pragmatic force can attach, and Wittgenstein, who looks at the smallest expressions whose utterance makes a move in the language game.) It is under this rubric that judgment is assimilated to action. A third Kantian idea is then to understand both judgment and action as the application of *concepts.* He does that by understanding concepts as the *rules* that determine what knowers and agents are responsible *for*—what they have committed themselves to.

I discuss the topics of my title—action, norms, and practical reasoning—in the idiom I developed in my book *Making It*

Explicit.[1] To begin with, I work within the context of what I call there a *normative pragmatics.* Specifically, I think of discursive practice as deontic scorekeeping: the significance of a speech act is how it changes what commitments and entitlements one attributes and acknowledges. I work also within the context of an *inferential semantics.* That is, discursive commitments (to begin with, doxastic ones) are distinguished by their specifically inferential articulation: what counts as evidence for them, what else they commit us to, what other commitments they are incompatible with in the sense of precluding entitlement to. This is a reading of what it is for the norms in question to be specifically *conceptual* norms. The overall idea is that the rationality that qualifies us as *sapients* (and not merely sentients) can be identified with being a player in the social, implicitly normative game of offering and assessing, producing and consuming, reasons.

I further endorse an *expressive* view of *logic.* That is, I see the characteristic role that distinguishes specifically logical vocabulary as being making explicit, in the form of a claim, features of the game of giving and asking for reasons in virtue of which bits of *non*logical vocabulary play the roles that they do. The paradigm is the *conditional.* Before introducing this locution, one can *do* something, namely, endorse an inference. After introducing the conditional, one can now *say* that the inference is a good one. The expressive role of the conditional is to make *explicit,* in the form of a claim, what before was *implicit* in our practice of distinguishing some inferences as good.

Giving and asking for reasons for *actions* is possible only in the context of practices of giving and asking for reasons generally—that is, of practices of making and defending *claims* or *judgments.* For giving a reason is always expressing a judgment: making a claim. So practical reasoning requires the availability of beliefs (doxastic commitments) as premises. On the side of the *consequences* of acquisition of practical deontic statuses, it appears in the essential role that propositional (assertible) contents play in specifying conditions of *success:* that is, what would count as fulfilling a commitment to act. Forming an intention (undertaking a commitment) to put a ball through a hoop requires knowing what it is to put a ball through a hoop—what must be *true* for that intention to *succeed.* This is a point about explanatory *autonomy:* I claim that one can explain the role of beliefs in theoretical reasoning (leading from claims to claims) without needing to appeal to practical reasoning, while I do not believe that one can do things in the opposite order.

II. The Approach

The treatment of action I am sketching is motivated by three truisms, and two more interesting ideas. First, beliefs make a difference both to what we *say* and to what we *do.* We license others to infer our beliefs (or, as I will say, our doxastic commitments) both from our explicit claims and from our overt intentional actions. Next is a (by now familiar) lesson we have been taught by Anscombe and Davidson.[2] Actions are performances that are intentional under some specification.[3] Such performances can genuinely be things *done* even though they have many specifications under which they are *not* intentional. Thus, alerting the burglar by flipping the switch was an action of mine, even though I did not intend to do that, because flipping the switch has another description, namely, "turning on the lights," under which it *was* intentional. A third, companion idea is that at least one way a specification of a performance can be privileged as one under which it is intentional is by figuring as the conclusion of a piece of practical reasoning that exhibits the agent's reasons for producing that performance.

Davidson's original idea was to eliminate *intentions* in favor of primary *reasons,* understood in terms of *beliefs* and *pro-attitudes* (paradigmatically, *desires*). My first idea is to start instead with normative statuses and attitudes corresponding to *beliefs* and *intentions.* I will try to explain *desires,* and, more generally, the pro-attitudes expressed by *normative* vocabulary, in terms of those beliefs and intentions. The thought is that there are two species of discursive commitment: the cognitive (or doxastic) and the practical. The latter are commitments to *act*. Acknowledgments of the first sort of commitment correspond to *beliefs*; acknowledgments of the second sort of commitment correspond to *intentions*. The first are takings-true, the second makings-true. Practical commitments are like doxastic commitments in being essentially inferentially articulated. They stand in inferential relations both among themselves (both means-end and incompatibility) and to doxastic commitments.

The second basic idea motivating the present account is that the noninferential relations between acknowledgments of practical commitments and states of affairs brought about by intentional *action* can be understood by analogy to the noninferential relations between acknowledgments of doxastic commitments and the states of affairs they are brought about by through conceptually contentful *perception*.

1. Observation (a discursive *entry* transition) depends on reliable dispositions to respond differentially to states of affairs of various kinds by acknowledging certain sorts of commitments, that is, by adopting deontic attitudes and so changing the score.

2. Action (a discursive *exit* transition) depends on reliable dispositions to respond differentially to the acknowledging of certain sorts of commitments, the adoption of deontic attitudes and consequent change of score, by bringing about various kinds of states of affairs.

Elaborating the first idea (modeling intention on belief as corresponding to inferentially articulated commitments) involves examining the sense in which practical reasons are *reasons*; elaborating the second idea (modeling action on perception, discursive exits on discursive entries) involves examining the sense in which practical reasons are *causes*. It is this latter idea that makes sense of the distinction, so crucial to Davidson, between acting *for* a reason and merely acting *with* a reason.

Put in terms of the deontic scorekeeping model of discursive practice, the idea is that *intentions* are to *reasons* as *commitments* are to *entitlements*. It follows that on this model, Davidson would be wrong to say that "someone who acts with a certain intention acts for a reason." For just as one can undertake doxastic or theoretical commitments to which one is not entitled by reasons, so one can undertake practical commitments to which one is not entitled by reasons. What makes a performance an *action* is that it is, or is produced by the exercise of a reliable differential disposition to respond to, the acknowledgment of a practical commitment. That acknowledgment need not itself have been produced as a response to the acknowledgment of other commitments inferentially related to it as entitlement-conferring reasons (though that it *could* be so elicited *is* essential to its being the acknowledgment of a practical commitment).

III. Three Patterns of Practical Reasoning

The strategy of trying to understand desires, and the pro-attitudes expressed by normative vocabulary more generally, in terms of their relation to beliefs and intentions—instead of the more orthodox Humean and Davidsonian strategy of starting with beliefs and desires—requires thinking about practical reasoning somewhat differently. Consider the following three bits of practical reasoning:

α. Only opening my umbrella will keep me dry, so I shall open my umbrella.

β. I am a bank employee going to work, so I shall wear a necktie.

γ. Repeating the gossip would harm someone, to no purpose, so I shall not repeat the gossip.

'Shall' is used here to express the significance of the conclusion as the acknowledging of a practical commitment. ('Will' would be used correspondingly to express a doxastic commitment to a prediction.)

The Davidsonian approach treats these as enthymemes, whose missing premises might be filled in by something like:

a. I want (desire, prefer) to stay dry.
b. Bank employees are obliged (required) to wear neckties.
c. It is wrong (one ought not) to harm anyone to no purpose.

(Orthodox contemporary Humeans would insist that something is missing in the second two cases, even when [b] and [c] are supplied. More on that thought later.) This enthymematic thesis is parallel on the side of practical reasoning to the insistence that theoretical reasoning be ˢcompletedˢ⁴ by the addition of conditionals, which assert the propriety of the material inferences involved, and transform the move into something that is *formally* valid. Sellars teaches us that that move is optional. We need not treat all correct inferences as correct in virtue of their form, supplying implicit or suppressed premises involving logical vocabulary as needed. Instead, we can treat inferences such as that from "Pittsburgh is to the west of Philadelphia" to "Philadelphia is to the east of Pittsburgh," or from "It is raining" to "The streets will be wet," as *materially* good inferences—that is, inferences that are good because of the content of their *non*logical vocabulary.⁵ I propose to adopt this nonformalist strategy in thinking about practical inferences.

One reason to do so was pointed out in the previous chapter: the notion of *formally valid* inferences is definable in a natural way from the notion of *materially correct* ones. The idea is to pick out some special subset of the vocabulary, and to observe features of inference that remain invariant when all other vocabulary is substituted for. In this way, the privileged vocabulary that is held fixed defines a notion of *form*. An inference is good in virtue of its form in this sense just in case it is a materially good inference and no materially bad inference results from it by substitutional transformations corresponding to replacing nonprivileged by nonprivileged vocabulary. If the form-defining fixed vocabulary is *logical* vocabulary, then the inferences whose propriety remains robust under such substitution are good in virtue of their *logical* form. On this substitutional approach, the notion of *logically* good inferences is explained in terms of a prior notion of *materially* good ones.

This account contrasts with the standard order of explanation, which treats all inferences as good or bad solely in virtue of their form, with the contents of the claims they involve mattering only for the truth of the (implicit) premises. According to this way of setting things out, there is no such thing as material inference. This view, which understands 'good inference' to mean 'formally valid inference', postulating implicit premises as needed, might be called a *formalist* approach to inference. It trades primitive goodnesses of inference for the truth of conditionals. I am not claiming that one *cannot* decide to talk this way. The point is just that one *need* not.

If one rejects the formalist order of explanation, what should one say about the role of conditional claims, such as "*If* Pittsburgh is to the west of Princeton, *then* Princeton is to the east of Pittsburgh"? The claim is that although such conditionals need not be added as explicit premises in order to license the inference from their antecedents to their consequents, they nonetheless serve to make explicit—in the form of a claim—the otherwise merely implicit endorsement of a material propriety of inference. Before we have conditionals on board, we can *do* something, namely, treat certain material inferences as correct. Once we have the expressive power of those logical locutions, we come to be able to *say that* they are good. The expressivist line about logic sees conditionals as making implicit material inferential commitments explicit, in the form of claims—but as *not* required to make the inferences they explicitate *good* inferences. Indeed, on this view, playing such an explicitating expressive role is precisely what distinguishes some vocabulary as distinctively *logical*.

IV. Material Properties of Practical Reasoning

I want to treat

A.
$$\frac{\text{It is raining}}{\therefore \text{ I shall open my umbrella.}}$$

as like

B.
$$\frac{\text{It is raining}}{\therefore \text{ The streets will be wet.}}$$

and say that *neither* one is an enthymeme.

The Davidsonian will respond that we can see that the reason offered in the first case is incomplete, because the inference would not go through if I did not want to stay dry. But I think that what we really know is rather that the inference would not go through if I had a *contrary* desire: say, the Gene Kelly desire to sing and dance in the rain, and so to get wet. But the fact that conjoining a premise incompatible with the desire to stay dry would infirm the inference (turn it into a bad one) does not show that the desire was all along already functioning as an implicit premise. There would be a case for that conclusion only if the reasoning involved were *monotonic*—that is, if the fact that the inference from p to q is a good one meant that the inference from p & r to q must be a good one. (So that the fact that the latter is *not* a good argument settled it that the former is not either.)

But material inference is not in general monotonic—even on the theoretical side. It can be in special cases, say, in mathematics and fundamental physics. But it never is in ordinary reasoning, and almost never in the special sciences. (Reasoning in clinical medicine, for instance, is resolutely nonmonotonic.) Consider the arguments that are codified in the following conditionals:

1. If I strike this dry, well-made match, then it will light. ($p \rightarrow q$)
2. If p and the match is in a very strong electromagnetic field, then it will *not* light. ($p \mathbin{\&} r \rightarrow \sim q$)
3. If p and r and the match is in a Faraday cage, then it will light. ($p \mathbin{\&} r \mathbin{\&} s \rightarrow q$)
4. If p and r and s and the room is evacuated of oxygen, then it will *not* light. ($p \mathbin{\&} r \mathbin{\&} s \mathbin{\&} t \rightarrow \sim q$)

The reasoning we actually engage in always permits the construction of inferential hierarchies with oscillating conclusions like this. A certain kind of formalist about logic will want to insist, for reasons of high theory, that material inference *must* be like formal inference in being monotonic. And at this point in the dialectic, such a *monotonous formalist* will invoke *ceteris paribus* clauses. I do not want to claim that invoking such clauses ("all other things being equal") is incoherent or silly. But we must be careful how we understand the expressive role they play. For they cannot (I want to say, "in principle") be cashed out; their content cannot be made explicit in the form of a series of additional premises. They are not shorthand for something we *could* say if we took the time or the trouble. The problem is not just that we would need an *infinite* list of the conditions being ruled out—though that is true. It is that the membership of such a list would be *indefinite:* we do not know how to specify in advance what belongs on the list. If we try to solve this problem by a *general* characterization, we get something equivalent to: "*ceteris paribus, q* follows from *p*" means that "*q* follows from *p* unless there is some *infirming* or *interfering* condition." But this is just to say that *q* follows from *p* except in the cases where for some reason it doesn't.

I would contend that *ceteris paribus* clauses should be understood as explicitly marking the nonmonotonicity of an inference, rather than as a deus ex machina that magically *removes* its nonmo-notonicity. The material inference (1) above is just fine as it stands. But if one wants explicitly to acknowledge that, even so, it can form the base of an oscillating hierarchy of inferences of the form of inference (2), (3), (4), and so on, then one can do so by refor-mulating it as

> 1′. If I strike this dry, well-made match, then *ceteris paribus* it will light.

Like their theoretical brethren, material proprieties of *practical* reasoning are nonmonotonic. So the fact that if I add "I want to get wet" as a second premise to inference (A) above, the resulting inference no longer goes through (that is, would be a bad one) does *not* show that the *denial* of that premise was already implicit. That would be the case only if material practical inferences were monotonic. For this reason, and to this extent, I am inclined to think that the sort of reductive Humeanism about practical rea-soning (about which more below) that recommends rational choice theory as an overarching theory of reasons generally is based on a mistaken philosophy of logic. In any case, as we will see, there is another way to go. We could think of the expressive role of avowals of desire as being analogous, on the practical side, to that of the conditional on the theoretical side: not as function-ing as a *premise,* but as making explicit the *inferential* commit-ment that permits the transition.

V. The Expressive Role of Normative Vocabulary

With this background, I can state my fundamental thesis: **norma-tive vocabulary** (including expressions of preference) **makes explicit the endorsement (attributed or acknowledged) of** *material* **proprieties of** *practical* **reasoning.** Normative vocabu-lary plays the same expressive role on the *practical* side that *condi-tionals* do on the *theoretical* side.

The idea is that the broadly normative or evaluative vocabulary used in (a), (b), and (c) ('prefer', 'obliged', and 'ought')—which Davidson understands as expressing the pro-attitudes needed to turn the incomplete reasons offered as premises in (α), (β), and (γ) into complete reasons—is used to make explicit in assertible, propositional form the endorsement of a *pattern* of material practical inferences. Different patterns of inference should be understood as corresponding to different sorts of norms or pro-attitudes.

For instance, an attributor who takes (α) to be entitlement-preserving will also take

a'. Only standing under the awning will keep me dry, so I shall stand under the awning.
a". Only remaining in the car will keep me dry, so I shall remain in the car.

and a host of similar inferences to have that status. Doing so is implicitly attributing a preference for staying dry. (Notice that because desires can compete, they provide only prima facie reasons for acting. Acknowledging the nonmonotonicity of practical reasoning, however, already provides for the features of reasoning that are normally dealt with by introducing such a notion.)

The norm, rule, or requirement that bank employees wear neckties is what makes going to work into a reason for wearing a necktie for bank employees. Taking it that there is such a norm or requirement also just is endorsing a pattern of practical reasoning: taking (β) to be a good inference for anyone who is a bank employee. This inferential pattern is different from that exhibited by (α) in two ways. First, there need not be for each interlocutor for whom (β) is taken to be a good inference a set of other inferences corresponding to (α), (α''), (α'). Instead, there will be related inferences such as

b'. I am a bank employee going to work, so I shall not wear a clown costume.
b". I am a bank employee going to work, so I shall comb my hair.

But these are licensed not by the norm made explicit in (b), but only by others associated with the same social institutional status (being a bank employee).

Second, the scorekeeper will take (β) to be a good inference for any interlocutor A such that the scorekeeper *undertakes* doxastic commitment to the claim that A is a bank employee—as opposed to *attributing* a desire or acknowledgment of a commitment. Here the norm implicitly underwriting the inference is associated with having a certain status, as employee of a bank, rather than with exhibiting a certain desire or preference. Whether one has a good reason to wear a necktie just depends on whether or not one occupies the status in question. This pattern, where what matters is the scorekeeper's undertaking of a commitment to A's occupying the status rather than A's acknowledgment of that commitment, corresponds to an *objective* sense of 'good reason for action' (according to the scorekeeper). In this sense, that A is preparing to go to work can be a good reason for A to wear a necktie, even though A is not in a position to appreciate it as such. (Compare the sense in which one's reliability as a reporter can entitle one to a claim—in the eyes of a scorekeeper—even if one is not aware that one is reliable, and so not aware of one's entitlement.)

Endorsement of practical reasoning of the sort of which (γ) is representative, codified in the form of a normative principle by (c), corresponds to an inferential commitment exhibiting a pattern different from those involved in either (α) or (β). For a scorekeeper who takes (γ) to be entitlement-preserving for A takes it to be entitlement-preserving for *anyone*, regardless of desires or preferences, and regardless of social status.

These *prudential* (or instrumental), *institutional*, and *unconditional* norms (made explicit by corresponding 'ought's) are meant only as three representative varieties, not as an exhaustive list. But they show how different sorts of norms correspond to different patterns of practical reasoning. The idea is that normative vocabulary is a kind of *logical* vocabulary, in my expressive sense:

its expressive function is to make explicit commitments to inferences.

To endorse a practical inference as entitlement-preserving is to take the doxastic premises as providing reasons for the practical conclusion. To exhibit a piece of good practical reasoning whose conclusion is a certain intention is to exhibit that intention, and the action (if any) that it elicits, as *rational,* as reasonable in the light of the commitments exhibited in the premises. Thus *all* of the 'ought's that make explicit species of practical reasoning taken as examples here, the prudential 'ought', the institutional 'ought', and the unconditional 'ought', are different kinds of *rational* 'ought'. There is no a priori reason to assimilate all such 'ought's to any one form—for instance, the prudential (Humean totalitarianism), as rationality-as-maximizing theorists (such as Gauthier) do. Recall also that the entitlement provided by prudential or institutional reasons need *not* be endorsed by the attributor; as Davidson points out, we need not take the agent's reasons to be *good* reasons.

From the point of view of this botanization of patterns of practical reasoning (which I do not pretend is complete), the humean and the kantian both have too restricted a notion of reasons for action. Each pursues a Procrustean order of explanation:

> The humean assimilates all reasons for action to the *first* pattern. Thus the humean will see the inferences like (β) and (γ) as incomplete, even with the addition of premises (b) and (c).
>
> The kantian assimilates all reasons for action to the *third* pattern.

The humean denies that a mere obligation or commitment could provide a reason for action, unless accompanied by some desire to fulfill it. And the kantian denies that a mere desire *(sinnliche Neigung)* could provide a reason for action, unless accompanied by the acknowledgment of some corresponding obligation or commitment.

VI. The Rational Will

A picture of the rational will emerges if we combine these three ideas:

the belief model of intending—the idea of modeling practical commitments on doxastic ones;

the picture of practical reasoning as relating beliefs as premises to intentions as conclusions; and

the modeling of actions as discursive exit transitions on perceptions as discursive entry transitions

It is important to remember to begin with acknowledging that a practical commitment is understood on the model *not* of *promising* but of *claiming*.[6] In particular, the commitment is not *to* anyone in particular, and one can change one's mind anytime, essentially without penalty. In both these respects, the practical commitments that correspond to intentions are like doxastic commitments rather than like promises. But while commitment *is* in force, it has consequences: for other practical commitments (and hence entitlements to practical commitments), via means-end reasoning and consideration of practical incompatibilities, and for doxastic commitments (and hence entitlement to doxastic commitments). Scorekeepers are licensed to infer our beliefs from our intentional actions (in context of course), as well as from our speech acts.

Acting with reasons is being *entitled* to one's practical commitments. Having this status is being intelligible to oneself and to others. This status can be vindicated by offering a suitable sample piece of practical reasoning (which need not actually have preceded the acknowledgment or performance in question). That piece of practical reasoning explains *why* one did as one did: what *reasons* one had. This means that in particular cases one can act intentionally but without reasons. But the capacity to acknowledge propositionally contentful practical commitments will be attributed only to those whose performances are largely intelligible.

The modeling of action on perception registers the crucial fact that acknowledgments of commitments can cause and be caused. Kant defines the rational will as the capacity to derive performances from conceptions of laws.[7] I am suggesting that we can replace "conception of a law" in this formulation by "acknowledgment of a commitment." "Law" is Kant's term for a binding rule—a norm. One's conception of a law is what one takes oneself to be obliged to do. Having a rational will, then, can be understood as having the capacity to respond reliably to one's acknowledgment of a commitment (of a norm as binding on one) by differentially producing performances corresponding to the content of the commitment acknowledged. But perception is strictly analogous on the input side. It is a capacity to respond differentially to the presence of, say, red things, by acknowledging a commitment with a corresponding content. The one capacity should in principle appear as no more mysterious than the other. According to this picture, we are rational creatures exactly insofar as our acknowledgment of discursive commitments (both doxastic and practical) makes a difference to what we go on to *do*.

Prior intentions are acknowledgments of practical commitments that are distinct from and antecedent to the responsive performances they are reliably differentially disposed to elicit. In other cases (intentions-in-action) the production of the performance may *be* the acknowledgment of the practical commitment. Prior intentions involve practical commitments to produce performances meeting *general* descriptions. Intentions-in-action are acknowledgments of practical commitments consisting of performances that are intentional under *demonstrative* specifications (e.g., "I shall jump *now*"). (These are Sellars's 'volitions'—"prior intentions whose time has come"[8]—a category rescued from the mistake of conceiving *tryings* as minimal *actions* that are safe in that they preclude the possibility of *failure*, just as, and for the same reasons, *seemings* are conceived as minimal *knowings* that are safe in that they preclude the possibility of *error*.)[9] One is a reliable agent (compare: reliable perceiver) with respect to a range of circumstances and a range of contents of practical commitments when one is so disposed that under those circumstances one's prior intentions with those contents conditionally *mature* into corresponding intentions-in-action.

One nice feature of this story is that what is expressed by the normative 'should' is related to what is expressed by the intentional 'shall' as third-person usage to first-person usage—that is, as attributing practical commitments (to others) is related to acknowledging practical commitments (oneself). The use of normative vocabulary such as 'should' expresses the attribution to an agent of commitment to a pattern of practical reasoning, while the use of 'shall' expresses acknowledgment by the agent of the sort of practical commitment that can appear as the conclusion of such practical reasoning. It is those acknowledgments that in competent agents are keyed to the production of the corresponding performances under favorable conditions. This relationship provides a way to make sense of weakness of the will (*akrasia*). For that phenomenon arises when self-*attributions* of practical commitments (which would be made explicit by statements of the form "I *should* . . .") do not have the causal significance of *acknowledgments* of practical commitments (which would be made explicit by statements of the form "I *shall* . . ."). In this form, the possibility of incompatible intentions is no more mysterious than that of incompatible claims (or, for that matter, promises). (This is an instance of a characteristic advantage of *normative* functionalisms over *causal* functionalisms.)

Notice that Davidson started off only with intentions-in-action—the case, on the present account, where the performance *is* the acknowledgment of a practical commitment. He later introduces intendings, but he construes them as judgments that some performance is "desirable, good, or what ought to be done."[10] Since he does not tell us what these normative terms mean, this is objectionably circular. By starting elsewhere, we have seen how to make independent sense of the expressive role of normative vocabulary.

Finally, notice that this account distinguishes:

a. acting intentionally, which is acknowledging a practical commitment, either in, or by producing, a corresponding performance
b. acting with reasons, which is being entitled to such a commitment
c. acting for reasons, which is the case where reasons are causes, when acknowledgment of practical commitment is elicited by proper reasoning

VII. Conclusion

I said at the outset that in this chapter I aimed to do three things:

to explain the expressive role that distinguishes specifically *normative* vocabulary, that is, to say what it is the job of such vocabulary to make explicit;
to introduce a non-humean way of thinking about *practical reasoning;* and
to offer a broadly kantian account of the *will* as a rational faculty of practical reasoning

by exploiting the structural analogies between discursive exit transitions in action and discursive entry transitions in perception to show how the rational will can be understood as no more philosophically mysterious than our capacity to notice red things. Although the account I have offered has of necessity been telegraphic, its goal has been to fulfill that discursive practical commitment.

THREE

◆ ◆ ◆

Insights and Blindspots
of Reliabilism

I. The Founding Insight of Reliabilism

One of the most important developments in the theory of knowledge in recent decades has been a shift in emphasis to concern with issues of the *reliability* of various processes of belief formation. One way of arriving at beliefs is more reliable than another in a specified set of circumstances just insofar as it is more *likely*, in those circumstances, to produce a *true* belief. Classical epistemology, taking its cue from Plato, understood knowledge as justified true belief (JTB). While Gettier had raised questions about the joint *sufficiency* of those three conditions, it is only more recently that their individual *necessity* was seriously questioned. What I call the 'Founding Insight' of reliabilist epistemologies is the claim that true beliefs can, at least in some cases, amount to genuine knowledge even where the justification condition is not met (in the sense that the candidate knower is unable to produce suitable justifications), provided the beliefs resulted from the exercise of capacities that are *reliable* producers of true beliefs in the circumstances in which they were in fact exercised.

The original motivation for the justification leg of the JTB epistemological tripod—for, in Plato's terminology, taking knowledge to require true opinion *plus an account*—is that merely *accidentally* true beliefs do not generally qualify as cases of knowledge. The man who guesses correctly which road leads to Athens, or who acquires his belief by flipping a coin, should not be said to *know* which is the correct road, even in the cases where he happens to be right. A space is cleared for reliabilism by the observation that supplying *evidence* for a claim, offering *reasons* for it, *justifying* it, are not the only ways in which to show that a belief is, if true, not true merely by accident. For that it suffices to show that the belief is of a kind that could, under the prevailing circumstances, have been *expected* or *predicted* to be true.[1] That the believer possesses good reasons for the belief is only one basis for such an expectation or prediction.

Consider an expert on classical Central American pottery who over the years has acquired the ability to tell Toltec from Aztec potsherds—reliably though not infallibly—simply by looking at them. We may suppose that there are no separately distinguishing features of the fragments that she can cite in justifying her classifications. When looking closely at the pieces, she just finds herself believing that some of them are Toltec and others Aztec. Suppose further that she regards beliefs formed in this way with great suspicion; she is not willing to put much weight on them, and in particular is not willing to risk her professional reputation on convictions with this sort of provenance. Before reporting to colleagues, or publishing conclusions that rest on evidence as to whether particular bits are Toltec or Aztec, she always does microscopic and chemical analyses that give her solid inferential evidence for the classification. That is, she does not believe that she is a reliable noninferential reporter of Toltec and Aztec potsherds; she insists on confirmatory evidence for beliefs on this topic that she has acquired noninferentially. But suppose that her colleagues, having followed her work over the years, have noticed that she is in fact a reliable distinguisher of one sort of pottery from the other. Her off-the-cuff inclinations to call something Toltec rather than Aztec can be trusted. It seems reasonable for them to say, in some case where she turned out to be right, that although she insisted on confirmatory evidence for her belief, in fact she *already knew* that the fragment in question was Toltec, even before bringing her microscope and reagents into play.[2]

If that is the right thing to say about a case of this sort, then knowledge attributions can be underwritten by a believer's *reliability*, even when the believer is not in a position to offer *reasons* for the belief. If they can be so underwritten, then justificatory internalism in epistemology is wrong to restrict attributions of knowledge to cases where the candidate knower can offer reasons inferentially justifying her (true) beliefs.[3] Reliabilism is a kind of epistemological *externalism*, for it maintains that facts of which a believer is not aware, and so cannot cite as reasons—for example, the reliability of her off-the-cuff dispositions to classify pot-sherds—can make the difference between what she believes counting as genuine knowledge and its counting merely as true belief.

So accepting the Founding Insight of reliabilism does involve disagreeing with the verdicts of justificatory internalism in some particular cases. But concern with reliability does not simply *contradict* the genuine insights of classical JTB epistemology. Rather, it can be seen as a *generalization* of the classical account. Reasoning takes its place as one potentially reliable process among others. Accepting only beliefs one *could* give reasons for—even if one did not acquire the belief inferentially by considering such reasons— is, under many circumstances, a reliable technique of belief formation. Where it is *not,* where the two criteria collide, it is arguable that the reliability criterion ought to trump the justificatory one. This might happen where inductive reasons could indeed be given for a belief, but where they are such weak reasons that the inference they underwrite falls short of reliability. Thus a colorful sunset may give some reason to believe that the next day will be fine ("Red at night, sailor's delight . . ."), even though acquiring one's weather beliefs on that basis may be quite unreliable. In such a case, even though one had a reason for what turned out to be a true belief, we might hesitate to say that one *knew* it would not rain. The reliability formula characterizes the role of such sources of knowledge as perception, memory, and testimony—none of which are immediately or obviously inferential in nature—at least as well as, and perhaps better than, a characterization of them in terms of looks, memories, and testimony offering *reasons*. That is because those sources *do* provide reasons sufficient for knowledge *at most* in the cases and the circumstances where they are reliable. Unreliable perception, memory, and testimony are *not* sufficient grounds for knowledge (and not for Gettier reasons).

What conclusions about the relations between reliability and reasons follow from what I have called the Founding Insight of reliabilism? The temptation is to suppose that for the reasons just considered, the concept of reliability of belief-forming processes can simply *replace* the concept of having good reasons for belief— that *all* the explanatory work for which we have been accustomed to call on the latter can be performed as well or better by the former. Thinking of things this way is thinking of the Founding Insight as motivating a recentering of epistemology. Classical JTB theories of knowledge had taken as central and paradigmatic exemplars true beliefs that the knower could justify inferentially. Beliefs that were the outcome of reliable processes of belief forma-tion—for instance, the noninferentially arrived-at deliverances of sense perception—qualified as special cases of knowledge just if the believer *knew* (or at least believed) that she was a reliable per-ceiver under those circumstances, and so could cite her reliability as a *reason* for belief. Reliability appeared as just one sort of reason among others. Reliabilist theories of knowledge take as their cen-tral and paradigmatic exemplars true beliefs that result from reli-able belief-forming mechanisms or strategies, regardless of the capacity of the believer to justify the belief, for instance, by citing her reliability. Believing what one can give reasons for appears as just one sort of reliable belief-forming mechanism among others.

More general theoretical considerations also seem to favor the replacement of the concept of reasons with that of reliability in epistemology. For we ought to ask why the concept of knowledge is of philosophical interest at all. It seems clear why we ought to care about the *truth* of beliefs, both our own and those of others. For the success of our actions often turns on the truth of the beliefs on which they are based.[4] But why should we in addition care about whatever feature distinguishes *knowledge* from mere true belief? Surely it is because we want to be able to *rely* on what others say, to provide us information. This interest in interpersonal communication of information motivates caring about the reliability of the processes that yield a belief independently of caring about its truth, for we can know something about the one in particular cases without yet knowing about the other. It is not wise to rely on lucky guesses. So independently of the vagaries of the prior epistemological tradition, and independently of how words like 'know' happen to be used in natural languages, we have a philosophical interest in investigating the status of beliefs that are produced by reliable processes. The capacity of a believer to provide reasons for her beliefs seems relevant to this story only at one remove: insofar as it contributes to reliability.

There are three distinguishable questions here. First, do the examples pointed to by the Founding Insight as genuine cases of knowledge stand up to critical scrutiny? For instance, ought we to count our pottery expert as having knowledge in advance of having reasons and in spite of her disbelief in her own reliability? Second, do such examples warrant a recentering of epistemology to focus on reliability of belief-forming processes rather than possession of reasons as distinctive of the most cognitively significant subclass of true beliefs? Third, does the possibility and advisability of such a recentering of epistemology mean that the explanatory role played by the concepts of reasons, evidence, inference, and justification can be taken over by that of reliable belief-forming processes—that is, that they matter *only* as marks of reliability of the beliefs they warrant? The temptation referred to above is the temptation to move from an affirmative answer to the first question to an affirmative answer to the other two. This is a temptation that should be resisted. I am prepared to accept the Founding Insight of reliabilism. But I will present reasons to dispute the recentering of epistemology from reasons to reliability to which it tempts us. And I will present further arguments to reject the replacement of the concept of reasons with that of reliability.

II. Chicken Sexing and Super Blindsight

To begin with, it is important to realize how delicate and special are the cases to which the Founding Insight appeals. If the expert not only *is* reliable but *believes* herself to be reliable, then she *does* have a reason for her belief, and issue is not joined with the justificatory internalist. Although the belief was acquired by noninferential perceptual mechanisms, it *could* in that case be justified inferentially. For that the shard is (probably) Toltec follows from the claim that the expert is perceptually disposed to call it 'Toltec', together with the claim that she is reliable in these matters under these circumstances. After all, to take the expert to be reliable just is to take it that the inference from her being disposed to call something 'Toltec' to its being Toltec is a good one. Thus, to get a case of knowledge based on reliability without reasons, we need one where a reliable believer does not take or believe herself to be reliable. These are going to be odd cases, since to qualify as even a candidate knower, the individual in question must nonetheless form a belief.

It is not hard to describe situations in which someone in fact reliably responds differentially to some sort of stimulus without having any idea of the mechanism that is in play. Industrial chicken-sexers can, I am told, reliably sort hatchlings into males and females by inspecting them, without having the least idea how they do it. With enough training, they just catch on. In fact, as I hear the story, it has been established that although these experts uniformly believe that they make the discrimination visually, research has shown that the cues their discriminations actually depend on are olfactory. At least in this way of telling the story, they are reliable noninferential reporters of male and female chicks, even though they know nothing about how they can make this discrimination, and so are quite unable to offer *reasons* (concerning how the chick looks or, a fortiori, smells) for believing a particular chick to be male. Again, individuals with blindsight are in the ordinary sense blind, and believe that they cannot respond differentially to visual stimuli. Yet they can, at least in some circumstances, reasonably reliably discriminate shapes and colors if forced to guess. Ordinary blindsight phenomena do not yield *knowledge,* since the individuals in question do not come to *believe* that, for instance, there is a red square in front of them. The most they will do is to *say* that, as a guess. For an example relevant to reliabilist concerns, we need a sort of super blindsight. Such super blindsight would be a phenomenon, first, in which the subject is more reliable than is typical for ordinary blindsight. For in the ordinary cases, the most one gets is a statistically significant preponderance of correct guesses relative to chance expectancy. Second, it would be a phenomenon in which the blindsighted individual formed an unaccountable *conviction* or belief that, for instance, there was a red square in front of him. Then we might indeed be tempted, as the Founding Insight urges, to say that the blindsighted individual actually *knew* there was a red square in front of him—just as the naive chicken-sexer *knows* that he is inspecting a male chick.

But as we saw already in connection with the archaeological expert, as so far described, these are cases that can cheerfully be accommodated within the framework of justificatory internalism. For though the examples have been carefully constructed so as to involve mechanisms of belief acquisition that are themselves *non*-inferential, this by itself does not entail that the candidate knowers cannot offer inferential justifications for those beliefs. An episte-mological internalism that denied the intelligibility of counting noninferentially acquired beliefs (paradigmatically, those acquired perceptually) as knowledge would be a nonstarter. Perceptual knowledge, according to any JTB account with any initial plausi-bility at all, depends on the capacity of the perceiver to offer justi-fying evidence from which the belief *could* have been inferred, even though in fact that is not how it came about. And the idea of reliability of a belief-forming process is exactly what is required to produce a recipe for such ex post facto justifications of noninfer-entially acquired beliefs.[5] In the standard case, we would expect that a reliable chicken-sexer would come to believe that he is reli-able. And that belief, together with his inclination to classify a particular chick as male, provides an appropriate inferential *justifi-cation* for the corresponding noninferentially acquired belief. So to put pressure on classical justificatory internalism, we need to build into the case the constraint that the candidate knower, though in fact reliable, does not believe himself to be reliable. This is perhaps most intuitive in the case of blindsight—even super blindsight—since it is characteristic of the original phenom-enon that the blindsighted continue to insist that they cannot see anything. They are, after all, blind.

At this point a tension comes to light. If the expert really does *not* take herself to be a reliable noninferential reporter of Toltec potsherds, one might think that it is cognitively irresponsible of her so much as to form the belief that a particular fragment is Toltec in advance of her investigation of microscopic and chemical evidence she *does* take to offer reliable indications. If the chicken-sexer does not believe that he is a reliable discriminator of male from female chicks (perhaps because he is still early in his training and does not yet realize that he has caught on), what business does he have coming noninferentially to *believe* that a particular chick is male, as opposed merely to finding himself inclined to say so, or putting it in the bin marked "M"? Again, *endorsing* that

inclination by coming to *believe* the chick is male seems irresponsible at this stage. If the super blindsighted person insists that he is
not a reliable reporter of red squares because he is blind and so
cannot *see* red squares, how can he at the same time nonetheless
genuinely *believe* that there is a red square in front of him? When
thus fully described, are the cases that motivate the Founding
Insight still coherent and intelligible?

I think that they are. There *is* a certain sort of cognitive irre-
sponsibility involved in those who do not take themselves to be
reliable reporters of a certain sort of phenomenon nonetheless
coming to believe the reports they find themselves inclined to
make. But I do not think that is a decisive reason to deny that it is
intelligible to acquire beliefs in this way. Cognitively irresponsible
beliefs can genuinely be beliefs. And in these very special cases,
such irresponsible beliefs can qualify as knowledge. At the very
least, I do not think it is open to the convinced justificatory internalist epistemologist to insist on the incoherence of examples
meeting the stringent conditions that have just been rehearsed.
For to be 'cognitively responsible' in the sense invoked in pointing to the tensions above just means not forming beliefs for which
one cannot offer any kind of a reason. Treating examples of the
sort sketched above as incoherent is in effect building this requirement into the definition of 'belief'—so that what one has acquired cannot count as a belief unless one is in a position to offer
at least some kind of reason for it. To impose that sort of requirement is surely to beg the question against the reliabilist epistemologist.

In fact, there is nothing unintelligible about having beliefs for
which we cannot give reasons. Faith—understood broadly as undertaking commitments without claiming corresponding entitlements—is surely not an incoherent concept. (Nor is it by any
means the exclusive province of religion.) And should the convictions of the faithful turn out not only to be true but also (unbeknownst to them) to result from reliable belief-forming processes,

I do not see why they should not be taken to constitute knowledge. The proper lesson to draw from the tension involved in the sorts of examples of knowledge to which the Founding Insight draws our attention, I think, is not that those examples are incoherent but that they are in principle exceptional. Knowledge based on reliability without the subject's having reasons for it[6] is possible as a local phenomenon, but not as a global one.

III. Epistemology and Semantics

What would it be like for *all* our knowledge, indeed, all our *belief,* to be like the examples we have been considering? Granted that cognitively irresponsible belief is possible in special, isolated cases, can we coherently describe practices in which people genuinely have beliefs, but *all* of them are cognitively irresponsible in that they are knowingly held in the absence of reasons for them? Put differently, do belief-forming practices of the sort that motivate the Founding Insight form an autonomous set—that is, a set of practices of belief formation that one could have though one had no others?

This is an important question in the context of the temptation to understand the significance of the Founding Insight of reliabilism as warranting a *recentering* of epistemology to focus on the reliability of belief-forming processes rather than on possession of reasons as what distinguishes the most philosophically interesting subclass of true beliefs. For the reason-giving practices that the classical justificatory internalist takes as paradigmatic ingredients of knowledge *are* autonomous in this sense. That is, we *can* make sense of a community whose members formed beliefs only when they thought they had justifications for them. Clearly all of their inferentially arrived-at beliefs can meet this condition. For the noninferentially acquired beliefs, we must insist only that they form *beliefs* noninferentially only in cases where they believe themselves to be reliable. *Those* beliefs can in turn have been acquired from others (who are and are taken already to be reliable), who train the novices in their discriminations. Thus children learn reliably to sort lollipops into piles labeled with color words first, and only once certified as reliable noninferential discriminators of colors do they graduate to forming *beliefs* of the form "That lollipop is purple." At that stage, if asked what reasons they have for those beliefs, they can invoke their own reliability. This invocation may be implicit, consisting, for instance, in saying something like, "I can tell what things are purple by looking at them." They might even say, "It looks purple to me," where this need be no more than a code for "I find myself inclined to sort it into the pile labeled 'purple'."[7]

It is at the very least unclear that we can make sense of a community of believers who, while often holding true beliefs, and generally acquiring them by reliable mechanisms, *never* are in a position to offer reasons for their beliefs. This would require that they never take themselves or one another to be reliable. For any attribution of reliability (when conjoined with a claim about what the reliable one believes or is inclined to say) *inferentially* underwrites a conclusion. A community precluded from giving reasons for beliefs cannot so much as have the concept of reliability—nor, accordingly (by anyone's lights), of knowledge. Its members can serve as measuring instruments—that is, reliable indicators—both of perceptible environing states and of one another's responses. But they cannot treat themselves or one another as doing that. For they do not discriminate between reliable indication and unreliable indication. Absent such discrimination, they cannot be taken to understand themselves or one another as *indicators* at all. For the very notion of a *correlation* between the states of an instrument and the states that it is a candidate for measuring is unintelligible apart from the assessments of reliability. Although they are reliable indicators, they do not in fact rely on their own or one another's indications, since they draw no conclusions from them.

I think these are good reasons to deny that what such reliable indicators have is knowledge. But the reasons forwarded thus far are at best probative, not dispositive. So far, however, our attention has been focused on the third condition on the concept of knowledge: whatever distinguishes it from mere true belief. If we shift our attention to the first condition—the condition that one does not know what one does not *believe*—stronger reasons to doubt the intelligibility of the reliability-without-reasons scenario emerge. For states that do not stand in inferential relations to one another, that do not serve as reasons one for another, are not recognizable as beliefs at all. The world is full of reliable indicators. Chunks of iron rust in wet environments and not in dry ones. Land mines explode when impressed by anything weighing more than a certain amount. Bulls charge red flapping bits of material. And so on. Their reliable dispositions to respond differentially to stimuli, and thereby to sort the stimuli into kinds, do not qualify as *cognitive*, because the responses that are reliably differentially elicited are not applications of *concepts*. They are not the formation of *beliefs*. Why not? What else is required for the reliable responses to count as beliefs? What difference makes the difference between a parrot trained to utter "That's red" in the presence of red things and a genuine noninferential reporter of red things who responds to their visible presence by acquiring the perceptual *belief that* there is something red in front of her?

At a minimum, I want to say, it is the *inferential articulation* of the response. Beliefs—indeed, anything that is propositionally contentful (whose content is in principle specifiable by using a declarative sentence or a 'that' clause formed from one), and so conceptually articulated—are essentially things that can serve as premises and conclusions of inferences. The subject of genuine perceptual beliefs is, as the parrot is not, responding to the visible presence of red things by making a potential move in a game of giving and asking for reasons: applying a concept. The believer is adopting a stance that involves further consequential commitments (for instance, to the object perceived as being colored) that is incompatible with other commitments (for instance, to the object perceived being green), and that one can show one's entitlements to in terms of other commitments (for instance, to the object perceived being scarlet). No response that is not a node in a network of such broadly inferential involvements, I claim, is recognizable as the application of *concepts*. And if not, it is not recognizable as a belief, or the expression of a belief, either.

We ought to respect the distinction between genuine perceptual *beliefs*—which require the application of *concepts*—and the reliable responses of minerals, mines, and matador fodder. I claim that an essential element of that distinction is the potential role as both premise and conclusion in reasoning (both theoretical and practical) that beliefs play. One might choose to draw this line differently, though I am not aware of a plausible competitor. But I do not think it is open to the reliabilist epistemologist to refuse to draw a line at all. To do that—not merely to broaden somewhat the third condition on knowledge, but to reject the first out of hand—is to change the subject radically. It is not to disagree about the analysis of knowledge but to insist on talking about something else entirely.[8]

If there is anything to this line of thought, then it is simply a mistake to think that the notion of being reliable could take over the explanatory role played by the notion of having reasons. For what distinguishes propositionally contentful and therefore conceptually articulated *beliefs,* including those that qualify as knowledge, from the merely reliable responses or representations of noncognitive creatures—those that have know-*how* but are not in the knowing-*that* line of work—is (at least) that they can both serve as and stand in need of *reasons.* I call the failure to realize this limitation on the explanatory powers of the concept of reliability the 'Conceptual Blindspot' of reliabilism.

That it is a mistake is at base a *semantic* point. But because of the *belief* condition on knowledge, it serves also to temper the conclusions we are entitled to draw from the Founding Insight of *epistemological* reliabilism concerning the *justification* condition. The examples of knowledge based on reliability without the possibility of offering reasons, which motivate the Founding Insight, are *essentially* fringe phenomena. Their intelligibility is parasitic on that of the reason-giving practices that underwrite ordinary ascriptions of knowledge—and indeed of belief *tout court*. Practices in which some beliefs are accorded the status of true and justified are autonomous—intelligible as games one could play though one played no other. Practices in which the only status beliefs can have besides being true is having been reliably produced are not autonomous in that sense. We must carefully resist the temptation to overstate the significance of the Founding Insight of reliabilism. Besides serving as a kind of reason, reliability can take a subordinate place alongside reasons in certifying beliefs as knowledge. But it cannot displace giving and asking for reasons from its central place in the understanding of cognitive practice.

IV. Reliabilism and Naturalism

So the proper domain of reliabilism is epistemology rather than semantics. Within epistemology, its proper lessons pertain to the condition that distinguishes knowledge from mere true belief. It does not provide the resources to distinguish the genus of which knowledge is a species—*conceptually* articulated, in particular *propositionally* contentful attitudes of *belief*—from the sorts of reliable indication exhibited by reliably indicating artifacts such as measuring instruments. Now, perhaps in pointing out that it would be a mistake to treat appeals to reliability as a candidate for replacing appeals to reasons in these broader explanatory domains I am attacking a straw man. The temptations to generalize the lessons of the Founding Insight to which I have been urging resistance may not be widely felt. Insofar as they are not, it would be tendentious to describe the merely notional possibility of such misguided overgeneralizations as constituting a flaw or blindspot in reliabilism itself—once the boundaries of that doctrine are suitably circumscribed.

However it may be with this temptation, there is another that is surely part and parcel of reliabilism's contemporary appeal in epistemology. That is the idea that reliabilism provides at least the raw materials for a *naturalized* epistemology—one that will let us exhibit states of knowledge as products of natural processes fully intelligible in broadly physicalistic terms. The strictures just rehearsed counsel us to take care in stating this ambition. Epistemological reliabilism suggests a path whereby *if* and *insofar as* the concept of (propositionally contentful) *belief* can be naturalized, so can the concept of *knowledge*. Reliabilism promises a recipe for extending the one sort of account to the other. The qualification codified in the antecedent of this conditional is not trivial, but neither is the conditional. In particular, it expresses a claim that convinced justificatory internalists might well have felt obliged to doubt. For if and insofar as what distinguishes knowledge from other true beliefs must be understood in terms of possession of *good reasons* or of justificatory *entitlement* or *warrant*, pessimism about the prospects for eventual naturalistic domestication of these latter normative notions would extend to the concept of knowledge itself.

A belief-forming mechanism is *reliable* (in specified circumstances), just in case it is objectively *likely* (in those circumstances) to result in *true* beliefs. If the notions of *belief* and *truth* have been explained physicalistically or naturalistically[9]—a substantive task, to be sure, but perhaps not a distinctively *epistemological* one—then one of the promises of reliabilism in epistemology is that all one needs to extend those accounts to encompass also *knowledge* is a naturalistic story about objective likelihood. But since it is *objective* likelihood that is at issue—and not subjective matters of conviction or evidence, of what else the subject knows or believes—such a story should not, it seems, be far to seek. For objective probabilities are a staple of explanations in the natural sciences, indeed, even in fundamental physics. The second conclusion the Founding Insight of reliabilism tempts us to draw is accordingly that it provides a recipe for a purely naturalistic account at least of what distinguishes knowledge from other true beliefs.

This line of thought is widely endorsed, even by those who do not applaud the project that motivates it. For it seems to me that even those who reject the premises that form its antecedent accept the conditional that *if* the concept of reliability can do the work previously done by notions of evidence or good reasons in distinguishing knowledge from merely true belief, and *if* naturalistic accounts of the concepts of *belief* and of *truth* are forthcoming, *then* a naturalistic account of knowledge is possible. That at least this *inference* is good is almost universally taken not only to be true but also to be *obviously* true. I think, however, that it is *not* a good inference. When we understand properly the sense in which facts about the reliability of a mechanism can be objective, we see that appeals to objective probability fall short of enabling fully naturalistic accounts of knowledge—even given the optimistic assumptions built into the premises of the inference. Seeing why this is so (in the next section of the chapter) provides the clues needed to formulate (in the final section) the lesson that we really ought to learn from the Founding Insight: what I will call the Implicit Insight of reliabilism.

V. Barn Facades and Goldman's Insight

The difficulty is a straightforward and familiar one, although I believe that its significance has not fully been appreciated. An objective probability can be specified only relative to a reference class. And in the full range of cognitive situations epistemological theories are obliged to address—by contrast to the carefully idealized situations described in artificially restricted vocabularies to which concepts of objective probability are applied in the special sciences—the world as it objectively is, apart from our subjective interests and concerns (paradigmatically, explanatory ones), does not in general privilege one of the competing universe of possible reference classes as the correct or appropriate one. Relative to a choice of reference class, we can make sense of the idea of objective probabilities, and so of objective facts about the reliability of various cognitive mechanisms or processes—facts specifiable in a naturalistic vocabulary. But the proper choice of reference class is not itself objectively determined by facts specifiable in a naturalistic vocabulary. So there is something left over.

The best way I know to make this point is by considering Alvin Goldman's barn facade example. This is perhaps ironic, because Goldman originally introduced the case in 1976 in a classic paper that demolished the pretensions of then-dominant *causal* theories of knowledge, precisely in order to make room for the sort of reliabilist alternatives that have held sway ever since.[10] While I do think this kind of example is decisive against causal theories of knowledge, in the context of aspirations to naturalize epistemology by appeal to considerations of reliability, it is a double-edged sword.

We are to imagine a physiologically normal perceiver, in standard conditions for visual perception (facing the object, in good light, no lenses or mirrors intervening, and so on), who is looking at a red barn. It looks like a red barn, he has seen many red barns before, and he is moved to say, and to believe, that there is a red barn in front of him. In fact, there is a red barn in front of him causing him perceptually to say and believe that. So his claim and his belief are true. He has the best reasons a perceiver could have for his belief: all the evidence he possesses confirms that it is a red barn and that he can see that it is. Of central importance to Goldman's original purpose is that we may suppose that the causal chain linking the perceiver to the red barn in front of him is ideal; it is just as such causal chains should be in cases of genuine perceptual knowledge. (We may not know how to formulate conditions on such chains necessary or sufficient to qualify them as knowledge, but whatever they may be, we are stipulating that those conditions are met in this case.) The perceiver has a true belief, has good reasons for that belief, and stands in the right causal relations to the object of his belief. Surely, one wants to say at this point, what he has in such a case is perceptual knowledge if anything is.

But things are less clear as we describe the case further, moving to facts *external* to the perceiver's beliefs, to his perceptual processing and to causal relations between the perceiver and what is perceived. For although the red barn our hero thinks he sees is indeed a red barn, it is, unbeknownst to him, located in Barn Facade County. There the local hobby is building incredibly realistic trompe l'oeil barn facades. In fact, our man is looking at the *only* real barn in the county—though there are 999 facades. These facades are so cunningly contrived that they are visually indistinguishable from actual barns. Were our subject (counterfactually) to be looking at one of the facades, he would form exactly the same beliefs he actually did about the real barn. That is, he would, falsely now, believe himself to be looking at an actual barn. It is just an accident that he happened on the one real barn.

The question is, does he know there is a red barn in front of him? A good case can be made that he does not. For though he has a true belief, it is only *accidentally* true. It is true only because he happened to stumble on the one real barn out of a thousand apparent ones. This seems to be a case of exactly the sort that the third condition on knowledge, the one distinguishing it from merely accidentally true beliefs, was introduced to exclude. If that is right—and I think it is—then it shows that classical justificatory epistemological internalism is inadequate.[11] It also shows that appeal to the causal chain linking the believer to what his belief is about is not adequate to distinguish knowledge from merely accidentally true belief—the surprising conclusion Goldman was originally after. For not only does the presence of barn facades in the vicinity—indeed, their local preponderance—not affect the beliefs the candidate knower can appeal to as evidence for or reasons justifying his belief, but it is also *causally* irrelevant to the process by which that belief was formed.

Goldman's positive conclusion, of course, is that the difference that makes the epistemological difference in such cases is that in the circumstances in which the belief was actually formed—that is, in Barn Facade County—the subject is not a *reliable* perceiver of barns. Forming a belief as to whether something is a barn by looking at it is not, in that vicinity, a reliable belief-forming mechanism. What is special about this case is just that the circumstances that render unreliable here what elsewhere would be a reliable process are *external* to the subject's beliefs and to their connection to their causal antecedents. Goldman took a giant step here. Both the critical argument and the positive suggestion he drew from it—the combination I call 'Goldman's Insight'—are epoch-making philosophical moves. But what is the exact significance of Goldman's reliabilist insight? Once we have rejected narrowly causal theories of the third condition on knowledge, and also classical justificatory internalist theories, what consequences should we draw from the demonstration of the positive bearing of external matters of reliability on assessments of knowledge? In particular, does Goldman's Insight support *naturalistic* ambitions in epistemology?

I think not. One of the happy features of Goldman's example is that it literalizes the metaphor of *boundaries* of reference classes. For suppose that Barn Facade County is one of a hundred counties in the state, all the rest of which eschew facades in favor of actual barns. Then, considered as an exercise of a differential responsive disposition within the *state* rather than within the county, our subject's process of perceptual belief formation may be quite reliable, and hence when it in fact yields correct beliefs, it may underwrite attributions of perceptual *knowledge*. But then, if the whole country, consisting of fifty larger states, shares the habits of

Barn Facade County—so that over the whole country (excepting this one state) facades predominate by a large margin—then considered as a capacity exercised in the *country,* the very same capacity will count as quite *un*reliable, and hence as insufficient to underwrite attributions of knowledge. And then again, in the whole *world,* barns may outnumber facades by a large margin. So considered with respect to that reference class, the capacity would once again count as reliable. And so on. Do we need to know about the relative frequencies of barns and facades in the solar system or the galaxy in order to answer questions about the cognitive status of our subject's beliefs? And yet, if instead of looking at ever broader reference classes we turn our attention to ever narrower ones, we end up with a reference class consisting simply of the actual exercise of the capacity in looking at a real barn. Within *that* reference class, the probability of arriving at a true belief is 1, since the unique belief arrived at in that situation is actually true. So with respect to the narrowest possible reference class, the belief-forming mechanism is maximally reliable.

Which is the correct reference class? Is the perceiver an objectively reliable identifier of barns or not? I submit that the facts as described do not determine an answer. Relative to each reference class there is a clear answer, but nothing in the way the world is privileges one of those reference classes, and hence picks out one of those answers. An argument place remains to be filled in, and the way the world objectively is does not, by itself, fill it in. Put another way, the reliability of the belief-forming mechanism (and hence the status of its true products as states of knowledge) varies depending on how we describe the mechanism and the believer. Described as apparently perceiving this barn, he is reliable and knows there is a barn in front of him. Described as an apparent barn-perceiver in this county, he is not reliable and does not know there is a barn in front of him. Described as an apparent barn-perceiver in the state, he is again reliable and a knower, while described as an apparent barn-perceiver in the country as a whole he is not. And so on. All these descriptions are equally true of him. All are ways of specifying his location that can equally be expressed in purely naturalistic vocabulary. But these naturalistically statable facts yield different verdicts about the perceiver's reliability, and hence about his status as a knower. And no naturalistically statable facts pick out one or another of these descriptions as uniquely privileged or correct. So the naturalistically statable facts do not, according to epistemological reliabilism, settle whether or not the perceiver is a knower in the case described.

Now, the case described is exceptional in many ways. Not every cognitive situation admits of descriptions in terms of nested, equally natural reference classes that generate alternating verdicts of reliability and unreliability. But I am not claiming that the idea of reliability is of no cognitive or epistemological significance. I am not denying Goldman's Insight. But situations with the structure of the barn facade example can arise, and they are counterexamples to the claim that reliabilism underwrites a naturalized epistemology—the mistaken idea that may be called the 'Naturalistic Blindspot' of reliabilism.

VI. Inference and the Implicit Insight of Reliabilism

How, then, *ought* we to understand the significance of considerations of reliability in epistemology? How can we properly acknowledge both the Founding Insight and Goldman's Insight while avoiding both the Conceptual and the Naturalistic Blindspot? And if not naturalism, what? *Super*naturalism? I think the key to answering these important questions is to see that, far from being opposed to considerations of what is a good reason for what, concern with reliability should itself be understood as concern with the goodness of a distinctive kind of *inference*. I will call this idea the 'Implicit Insight' of epistemological reliabilism.

Epistemology is usually thought of as the theory of knowledge. But epistemological theories in fact typically offer accounts of when it is proper to *attribute* knowledge: for instance, where there is justified true belief, or where true beliefs have resulted from reliable belief-forming processes. Now, a theory of knowledge can take this form. The two might be related as formal to material mode, in Carnap's terminology; instead of asking what X's are, we ask when the term 'X' is properly applied. But the two need not be versions of the same question. In the case of knowledge, I think they stand in a more complex relationship.

What is one doing in taking someone to have knowledge? The traditional tripartite response surely has the right form. To begin with, one is attributing some sort of *commitment:* a belief. For the reasons indicated above in connection with the Conceptual Blindspot, I think that being so committed must be understood as taking up a stance in an *inferentially* articulated network—that is, one in which one commitment carries with it various others as its inferential consequences and rules out others that are incompatible. Only as occupying a position in such a network can it be understood as *propositionally* (and hence *conceptually*) contentful. Corresponding to the traditional justification condition on attributions of knowledge, we may say that not just any commitment will do. For it to be *knowledge* one is attributing, one must also take the commitment to be one the believer is in some sense *entitled* to. Mindful of the Founding Insight, we need not assume that the only way a believer can come to be entitled to a propositionally contentful commitment is by being able to offer an inferential justification of it. Instead, entitlement may be attributed on the basis of an assessment of the reliability of the process that resulted in the commitment's being undertaken. We will return to look more closely at attributions of reliability, our final topic, just below.

So to take someone to know something, one must do two things: attribute a certain kind of inferentially articulated *commitment,* and attribute a certain kind of *entitlement* to that commitment.[12] But not all beliefs to which the believer is entitled count as knowledge. One takes them so to qualify only where one takes them in addition to be *true*. What is it to do that? Taking a claim or belief to be true is not attributing an especially interesting and mysterious property to it; it is doing something else entirely. It is *endorsing* the claim oneself. Spurious metaphysical problems concerning the property of truth are what one gets if one *mis*-understands what one is doing in *adopting* a stance oneself—under-taking a commitment—on the model of *describing, characterizing,* or *attributing* a property to someone *else*'s commitment. A corre-sponding mistake would be to think of making a promise, for instance, that one would drive one's friend to the airport, as attributing a special sort of property to the proposition that one will drive one's friend to the airport—a property whose rela-tion to one's own motivational structure will then cry out for explanation.

In calling what someone has 'knowledge', one is doing three things: *attributing* a *commitment* that is capable of serving both as premise and as conclusion of inferences relating it to other commitments, *attributing entitlement* to that commitment, and *undertaking* that same commitment oneself.[13] Doing this is adopting a complex, essentially *socially* articulated stance or posi-tion in the game of giving and asking for reasons. I will not attempt to develop or defend this way of understanding knowl-edge as a normative social status here; I have done so at length in *Making It Explicit*.[14] I have sketched it here because of the per-spective it gives us on the role of attributions of *reliability* in securing entitlement to beliefs.

For suppose that, in the same spirit in which we just asked what one is *doing* in taking someone to be a knower, we ask what one is *doing* in taking someone to be a *reliable* former of noninferential beliefs about, say, red barns in front of him. To take someone to be a reliable reporter of red barns, under certain circumstances, is to take it that his reports of barns, in those circumstances, are likely to be *true*. According to the account just offered, to do that is to be inclined to *endorse* those reports oneself. And that means that what one is doing in taking someone to be reliable is endorsing a distinctive kind of *inference:* an inference, namely, from the *attribution* to another of a propositionally contentful commitment acquired under certain circumstances to the *endorsement* or *undertaking* oneself of a commitment with that same content. Inferences exhibiting this socially articulated structure are *reliability inferences.* Endorsing such an inference is just what being prepared to *rely* on someone else as an informant consists in: being willing to use *his* commitments as premises in one's *own* inferences (including practical ones).

The possibility of extracting information from the remarks of others is one of the main points of the practice of assertion, and of attributing beliefs to others. So reliability inferences play an absolutely central role in the game of giving and asking for reasons—indeed, every bit as central as the closely related but distinguishable assessments of the *truth* of others' claims and beliefs. That concern with reliability is not opposed to concern with what is a reason for what, but actually a crucially important species of it, is what I want to call the Implicit Insight of reliabilism. Reliabilism deserves to be called a form of epistemological *externalism,* because assessments of reliability (and hence of knowledge) can turn on considerations external to the reasons possessed by the candidate knower himself. In those cases, such assessments concern the reasons possessed by the *assessor* of knowledge rather than by the *subject* of knowledge. The lesson I want to draw is that they should not therefore be seen as external to the game of giving and asking for reasons, nor to concern with what is a reason for what. Reliabilism points to the fundamental *social* or *interpersonal* articulation of the practices of reason giving and reason assessing within which questions of who has knowledge arise.

A final dividend that this way of thinking about reliability pays is that it permits us to see what is really going on in the barn facade cases, and so how to take on board Goldman's Insight. For the relativity to reference class of assessments of reliability (and hence of knowledge) that seemed so puzzling when viewed in a context that excluded concern with what is a reason for what falls naturally into place once we understand assessments of reliability as issues of what *inferences* to endorse. The different reference classes just correspond to different (true) collateral premises or auxiliary hypotheses that can be conjoined with the attribution of noninferentially acquired perceptual belief in order to extract inferential consequences the assessor of reliability (and knowledge) can use as premises in her *own* inferences. From the perceiver's report of a red barn and the premise that he is located in Barn Facade County, there is *not* a good inference to the conclusion that there is a red barn in front of him. From the perceiver's report and the premise that he is located in the *state,* there *is* a good inference to that conclusion. From the report and the premise that he is located in the *country,* there is not a good inference to that conclusion. And so on. All those collateral premises are true, so there are a number of candidate reliability inferences to be assessed. But there is no contradiction, because they are all *different* inferences. Nothing spooky or supernatural is going on—of course. The relativity to description that is threatening to an understanding of reliability and knowledge that ignores reason giving, justification, and inference can be taken in stride once we see concern with reliability as arising in just such contexts. For we expect the goodness of inferences to be sensitive to differences in how the items we are reasoning about are described. The intensionality of assessments of reliability is just a mark of their membership in the inferential order rather than the causal order. And we saw in the previous chapter, we should expect material inferences of this sort to be nonmonotonic.

To avoid the Conceptual Blindspot, one must appreciate the significance of specifically *inferential* articulation in distinguishing representations that qualify as *beliefs,* and hence as candidates for knowledge. To avoid the Naturalistic Blindspot, one must appreciate that concern with reliability is concern with a distinctive interpersonal *inferential* structure. Appreciating the role of inference in these explanatory contexts is grasping the Implicit Insight of reliabilism. It is what is required to conserve and extend both the Founding Insight and Goldman's Insight without being crippled by the difficulties into which they tempt us.

FOUR

What Are Singular Terms, and Why Are There Any?

I. What Are Singular Terms?

1. Singular Terms and Objects

What conditions on the use of an expression are necessary and sufficient for it to be functioning as or playing the role of a singular term? What sort of expressive impoverishment is a language condemned to by not having anything playing that sort of role? The answers to these questions may seem straightforward, at least in the large. Singular terms are linguistic expressions that refer to, denote, or designate particular objects.[1] The point of having something playing this role in linguistic practice is to make it possible to talk about particular objects, which, together with their properties and relations, make up the world in which the practice is conducted.

The first of these claims may be accepted without accepting the order of explanation presupposed by the transition from the first claim to the second. To begin with, it may be questioned whether the concept *particular object* can be made intelligible without appeal to the concept *singular term*. Frege, for instance, implicitly denies this when in the *Grundlagen* he explains the ontological category of particular objects, to which he is concerned to argue numbers belong, in effect as comprising whatever can be referred to by using singular terms, to which linguistic category he argues numerals belong.

Put somewhat more carefully, the first answer forwarded above must be: singular terms are expressions that, in Quine's useful phrase "*purport* to refer to just one object." Quine is suspicious of the full-blooded notions of representational purport implicit in intentional idioms, and the echoes in his phrase are a reminder of his desire to explain much of what they might be thought to explain by appeal to more austere linguistic analogs. For singular referential purport, in the sense he appeals to, need not be an intentional affair. As Quine is quick to point out, "Such talk of purport is only a picturesque way of alluding to the distinctive grammatical role that singular . . . terms play in sentences."[2] The real task is to specify this role. Explanatory ground is gained by appeal to the principle Quine states only in the presence of such an account. That story, however, would offer a direct answer to the question "What is a singular term?"—one that does not appeal to (but on the contrary can itself be used via Quine's principle to help explain) the dark and pregnant notion of referential or representational purport. It is such an account that I aim to provide in the remainder of this chapter.

2. Subsentential Expressions and Projecting the Use of Novel Sentences

The pre-Kantian tradition took it for granted that the proper order of semantic explanation begins with a doctrine of concepts or terms, divided into singular and general, whose meaningfulness can be grasped independently of and prior to the meaningfulness of judgments. Appealing to this basic level of interpretation, a doctrine of judgments then explains the combination of concepts into judgments, and how the correctness of the resulting judgments depends on what is combined and how. Appealing to this derived interpretation of judgments, a doctrine of consequences finally explains the combination of judgments into inferences, and how the correctness of inferences depends on what is combined and how. Kant rejects this. One of his cardinal innovations is the claim that the fundamental unit of awareness or cognition, the minimum graspable, is the judgment. For him, interpretations of something as classified or classifier (term or predicate) make sense only as remarks about its role in judgment. In the *Grundlagen,* Frege follows this Kantian line in insisting that "only in the context of a proposition [*Satz*] does a name have any meaning."[3] Frege takes this position because it is only to the utterance of sentences that pragmatic force attaches, and the explanatory purpose of associating semantic content with expressions is to provide a systematic account of such force.

Since semantics must in this way answer to pragmatics, the category of sentences has a certain kind of explanatory priority over subsentential categories of expression, such as singular terms and predicates. For sentences are the kind of expression whose free-standing utterance (that is, whose utterance unembedded in the utterance of some larger expression containing it) has the pragmatic significance of performing a speech act. Declarative sentences are those whose utterance typically has the significance of an assertion, of making a claim. Accordingly, there is available a sort of answer to the questions "What are sentences, and why are there any?" that is not available for any subsentential expression: Sentences are expressions whose unembedded utterance performs a speech act such as making a claim, asking a question, or giving a command. Without expressions of this category, there can be no speech acts of any kind, and hence no specifically linguistic practice.

From this point of view it is not obvious why there should be subsentential expressions at all, for they cannot have the same sort of fundamental pragmatic role to play that sentences do. So we ought to start by asking a question more general than that of the subtitle of this chapter: "What are subsentential expressions, and why are there any?" Given the pragmatic priority of sentences, why should other semantically significant categories be discerned at all? Sentences are assigned semantic contents as part of an explanation of what one is doing in asserting them, what one claims, what belief one avows thereby. But the utterance of an essentially subsentential expression, such as a singular term, is not the performance of this sort of speech act. It does not by itself make a move in the language game, does not alter the score of commitments and attitudes that it is appropriate for an audience to attribute to the speaker. Accordingly, such expressions cannot have semantic contents in the same sense in which sentences can. They cannot serve as premises and conclusions of *inferences.* They can be taken to be semantically contentful only in a derivative sense, insofar as their occurrence as components in sentences contributes to the contents (in the basic, practice-relevant inferential sense) of those sentences.

If, because of their pragmatic priority, one begins rather with the semantic interpretation of sentences, what is the motivation for decomposing them so as to interpret subsentential expressions as well? Why recognize the semantically significant occurrence of expressions of any category other than sentences? Frege begins one of his later essays with this response: "It is astonishing what language can do. With a few syllables it can express an incalculable number of thoughts, so that even a thought grasped by a human being for the very first time can be put into a form of words which will be understood by someone to whom the thought is entirely new. This would be impossible, were we not able to distinguish parts in the thought corresponding to parts of a sentence."[4]

The ability to produce and understand an indefinite number of novel sentences is a striking and essential feature of linguistic practice. As Chomsky has since emphasized, such creativity is the rule rather than the exception. Almost every sentence uttered by an adult native speaker is being uttered for the first time—not just the first time for that speaker, but the first time in human history. This high proportion of sentential novelty appears in surveys of empirically recorded discourses, and becomes evident on statistical grounds when one compares the number of sentences of, say, thirty or fewer words with the number there has been time for English speakers to have uttered, even if we never did anything else.[5] "Please pass the salt" may get a lot of play, but it is exceptionally unlikely that a sentence chosen at random from this book, for instance, would ever have been inscribed or otherwise uttered by someone else.

The point is often made that individual speakers in training are exposed to correct uses only of a relatively small finite number of sentences, and must on that basis somehow acquire practical mastery, responsive and productive, of proprieties of practice governing an indefinitely larger number.[6] The need to explain the possibility of projecting proper uses for many sentences from those for a few is not just a constraint on accounts of language learning by individuals, however. For what is of interest is not just how the trick (of acquiring practical linguistic competence) might be done, but equally what the trick consists in, what counts as doing it. As I just remarked, the whole linguistic community, by the most diachronically inclusive standards of community membership, has only produced (as correct) or responded to (as correct) a set of sentences that is small relative to the set of sentences one who attributes to them a language is thereby obliged to take it they have somehow determined correct uses for. The idea that there is a difference between correct and incorrect uses of sentences no one has yet used involves some sort of projection.

We are well advised to follow Frege in taking seriously the fact that the sentences we are familiar with do, after all, have parts. A two-stage compositional strategy for the explanation of projection would take it that what is settled by proprieties of use governing the smaller, sample set of sentences, which is projected, is the correct use of the subsentential components into which they can be analyzed or decomposed. The correct use of these components is then to be understood as determining the correct use also of further combinations of them into novel sentences.[7] The linguistic community determines the correct use of some sentences, and thereby of the words they involve, and so determines the correct use of the rest of the sentences that can be expressed by using those words. (Notice that I am talking about projecting *proprieties* governing some sentences from *proprieties* governing others, *not* about projecting any of those proprieties from nonnormatively characterized *dispositions*.)

The need to project a distinction between proper and improper use for novel sentences provides the broad outlines of an answer to the question "What are subsentential expressions for?" or "Why are there any subsentential expressions?" But what *are* subsentential expressions, functionally? According to the two-stage explanatory scheme, there are two sorts of constraints on the correct use of subsentential expressions, corresponding to their decompositional and compositional roles, respectively. Their correct use must be determined by the correct use of the relatively small subset of the sentences in which they can appear as components, and their correct use must collectively determine the correct use of all the sentences in which they can appear as components.

The key to the solution Frege endorses is the notion of *substitution*. For the first, or decompositional stage, sentences are to be analyzed into subsentential components by being assimilated as substitutional variants of one another—that is, related by being substitutionally accessible one from another. Regarding two sentences as substitutional variants of each other is discerning in them applications of the same function, in Frege's sense. In the second, or recompositional stage, novel sentences (and their interpretations) are to be generated as applications of familiar functions to familiar substitutable expressions. Familiar sorts of substitutional variation of familiar classes of sentences result in a host of unfamiliar sentences. It is this substitutional clue to the nature of subsentential expressions and their interpretation that is pursued in what follows.

II. What Are Singular Terms?

1. Syntax: Substitution-Structural Roles

First let me talk about *syntax*. "What are singular terms?" The question has been posed from the point of view of someone who understands (or is prepared to pretend to understand) already what it is to use an expression as a sentence, but admits to puzzlement concerning the distinctive contribution made by the occurrence of singular terms in such sentences. One way to get into this situation[8] is to begin with a pragmatics, an account of the significance of some fundamental kinds of speech act. A line can then be drawn around the *linguistic* by insisting that for the acts in question to qualify as *speech* acts, the fundamental kinds must include *asserting*. A general pragmatic theory then specifies for each speech act the circumstances in which, according to the practices of the linguistic community, one counts as entitled or obliged to perform it, and what difference that performance makes to what various interlocutors (the performers included) are thereby entitled or obliged to do. Assertional performances (and thereby specifically linguistic practices) are in turn picked out by *inferential* articulation: the way in which the pragmatic circumstances and consequences of acts of asserting depend on the inferential relations of ground and consequent among sentences. The category of sentences is then defined as comprising the expressions whose (freestanding or unembedded) utterance standardly has the significance of performing a speech act of one of the fundamental kinds. A pair of sentences[9] may be said to have the same pragmatic potential if across the whole variety of possible contexts their utterances would be speech acts with the same pragmatic significance (Fregean force).

Frege's notion of *substitution* can then be employed again to define subsentential categories of linguistic expression. Two subsentential expressions belong to the same syntactic or grammatical category just in case no well-formed sentence (expression that can be used to perform one of the fundamental kinds of speech act) in which the one occurs can be turned into something that is not a sentence merely by substituting the other for it. Two subsentential expressions of the same grammatical category share a semantic content just in case substituting one for the other preserves the pragmatic potential of the sentences in which they occur. Then the intersubstitution of co-contentful subsentential expressions can be required to preserve the semantic contents of the sentences (and other expressions) they occur in. In this way, the notion of substitution allows both syntactic and semantic equivalence relations among expressions to be defined, beginning only with an account of force or pragmatic significance. The relations differ only in the substitutional invariants: expressions assimilated accordingly as well-formedness is preserved by intersubstitution share a syntactic category; those assimilated accordingly as pragmatic potential is preserved share a semantic content.

There are three sorts of roles that expression kinds can play with respect to this substitutional machinery. An expression can be substituted *for,* replacing or being replaced by another expression, as a component of a compound expression. An expression can be substituted *in,* as compound expressions in which component expressions (which can be substituted for) occur. Finally, there is the substitutional frame or remainder: what is common to two substituted-in expressions that are substitutional variants of each other (corresponding to different substituted-for expressions): '$q \rightarrow r$' results from '$p \rightarrow r$', by substituting 'p' for 'q'. The substitutional frame that is common to the two substitutional variants may be indicated by '$\alpha \rightarrow r$', in which 'α' marks a place where an appropriate substituted-for expression would appear.

Being substituted in, substituted for, or a substitutional frame are the *substitution-structural roles* that (sets of) expressions can play. The relation *being a substitutional variant of* obtains between substituted-in expressions, which must accordingly already have been discerned. Substitutional variation is indexed by pairs of expressions that are substituted for, which accordingly also must be antecedently distinguishable.[10] Substitution frames, by contrast, are not raw materials of the substitution process; they are its products. To discern the occurrence of a substitution frame, for instance, '$\alpha \to r$' in '$p \to r$', is to conceive of '$p \to r$' as paired with the set of all of its substitutional variants, such as '$q \to r$'. These are available only after a substitution relation has been instituted. For this reason, being substituted for and being substituted in may be said to be *basic* substitution-structural roles, while being a substitution frame is a (substitutionally) *derived* substitution-structural role.

Frege was the first to use distinctions such as these to characterize the roles of singular terms and predicates. Frege's idea is that predicates are the substitutional sentence frames formed when singular terms are substituted-for in sentences.[11] That is why predicates do, and singular terms do not, have argument places and fixed adicities. But it is clear that playing the substitution-structural roles of substituted-for and frame with respect to substitutions in sentences is not by itself sufficient to permit the identification of expressions as singular terms and predicates, respectively. For, as in the schematic example of the previous paragraph, what is substituted for may be sentences rather than singular terms, and the frames exhibited by substitutionally variant (sets of) sentences thereby become sentential connectives or operators rather than predicates.[12] The substitution-structural roles do provide important necessary conditions for being singular terms and predicates, though.

Why not think of predicates also as expressions that can be substituted for? If "Kant admired Rousseau" has "Rousseau admired Rousseau" as a substitutional variant when the category substituted for is terms, does it not also have "Kant was more punctual than Rousseau" as a substitutional variant when the category substituted for is predicates? Indeed, doesn't talk about predicates as a category of expression presuppose the possibility of such replacement of one predicate by another, given the substitutional definition of 'category' offered above? It does; but though either notion can be used to assimilate expressions accordingly as it preserves well-formedness of sentences, it is important to distinguish between *substituting* one expression for another and *replacing* one sentence frame with another.

To begin with, it should not be forgotten that the frames on which replacement operates must themselves be understood as products of the former sort of substitution operation. What play the substitutionally derivative roles, for instance, of sentence frames, can be counted as *expressions* only in an extended sense. They are more like *patterns* discernible in sentential expressions, or sets of such expressions, than like parts of them. Sentence frames are what Dummett calls *complex* predicates, not *simple* ones. A sentence frame is not a prior constituent of a sentence but a product of analyzing it, in particular by assimilating to other sentences related to it as substitutional variants, when one or more of its actual constituents is substituted for. As a result, relative to such an analysis a sentence can exhibit many occurrences of expressions that can be substituted for, but only one frame resulting from such substitutions. A further difference, which is also a consequence of the substitutionally derivative status of sentence frames, is that replacing sentence frames, or more generally discerning substitutional variants in the second, wider, sense, which involves replacement of derived categories, requires matching argument places and keeping track of cross-referencing among them.[13] This has no analog in substitution for expressions of substitutionally basic categories. So although replacement of derivative expressions is sufficiently like substitution for basic expressions to define syntactic equivalence classes of expressions, they differ in ways that will later be seen to be important.

2. Semantics: Substitution-Inferential Significances

Now let me say something about *semantics*. Following the line of thought introduced in Chapter 1 gives us the clue that raising the issue of the *inferential* significance of the occurrence in a sentence of some kind of subsentential expression is what shifts concern from the syntactic consequences of substitutional relations to their specifically semantic significance.

Inferences that relate substitutionally variant substituted-in sentences as premise and conclusion may be called *substitution inferences*. An example is the inference from

Benjamin Franklin invented bifocals

to

The first postmaster general of the United States invented bifocals.

The premised sentence is substituted *in,* and a singular term is substituted *for,* to yield the conclusion. Because Benjamin Franklin was the first postmaster general of the United States, the inference from the premise to its substitutional variant is truth-preserving: in the appropriate context, commitment to the premise involves commitment to the conclusion.

The substitution inference above *materially involves* the particular singular terms that occur (and are substituted for) in it. The particular predicate is not materially involved. For it is possible to replace that predicate with others without affecting the correctness (in this case, status-preservingness) of the inference. Thus if "α invented bifocals" is replaced by "α walked," the substitution inference from

Benjamin Franklin walked

to

The first postmaster general of the United States walked

will be correct under the same assumptions as the original.

The idea of replacing substitutional frames permits, for instance, the substitution instances quantified over in "Anyone who admires someone admires himself," such as

Rousseau admires Montaigne and Rousseau admires Rousseau

to appear as *frame-variants* of

Rousseau writes about Montaigne and Rousseau writes about Rousseau,

when "α admires β and α admires α" is replaced by "α writes about β and α writes about α." The notion of substitution inference may be broadened to include inferences whose conclusion results from the premise upon replacement of a substitutional frame or pattern it exhibits. That is, the conclusions of inferences to be called 'substitution inferences' may be *either* frame variants or strict substitutional variants of the premises (corresponding to basic and derived substitutional variation).

The substitution inferences (in this broad sense) in which singular terms are materially involved differ in their formal structure from the substitution inferences in which predicates are materially involved. This difference provides another way of distinguishing the characteristic role of singular terms from that of other subsentential expressions, paradigmatically predicates. The point is noted by Strawson (in *Subject and Predicate in Logic and Grammar*), who observes that predicates, but not singular terms, stand in "one-way inferential involvements." If the inference from "Benjamin Franklin walked" to "The inventor of bifocals walked" is a good one, then so is that from "The inventor of bifocals walked" to "Benjamin Franklin walked." Substitutions for singular terms yield reversible inferences. But it does not follow that the inference from "Benjamin Franklin moved" to "Benjamin Franklin walked" is a good one just because the inference from "Benjamin Franklin walked" to "Benjamin Franklin moved" is a good one. Replacements of predicates need not yield reversible inferences. Substitution inferences materially involving singular terms are de jure symmetric, while all predicates are materially involved in some asymmetric substitution inferences (though they may be involved in some symmetric ones as well).

One way to think about this difference is that where the goodness of a substitution inference is defined by its preservation of some semantically relevant whatsit, reflexivity and transitivity of those inferences is guaranteed by the nature of the preservation relation. The stuttering inference from p to p preserves any status that p might be accorded, while if the inference from p to q preserves that status, and that from q to r preserves it, then so must that from p to r. The symmetry of the relation, however, is assured neither by its status as an inferential relation nor by its holding accordingly as some status of the premise is preserved or transmitted[14] to the conclusion. Predicate substitution inferences may be asymmetric, while singular term substitution inferences are always symmetric.

So singular terms are grouped into equivalence classes by the good substitution inferences in which they are materially involved, while predicates are grouped into reflexive, transitive, *a*symmetric structures or families. That is to say that some predicates are simply inferentially weaker than others, in the sense that everything that follows from the applicability of the weaker one follows also from the applicability of the stronger one, but not vice versa. The criteria or circumstances of appropriate application of '. . . walks' form a proper subset of those of '. . . moves'. Singular terms, by contrast, are not materially involved in substitution inferences whose conclusions are inferentially weaker than their premises.[15] To introduce a singular term into a language, one must specify not only criteria of application but also criteria of identity, specifying which expressions are intersubstitutable with it.

Each member of such an inferential interchangeability equivalence class provides, symmetrically and indifferently, both sufficient conditions for the appropriate application and appropriate necessary consequences of application for each of the other expressions in the class.[16] So, when the material substitution-inferential commitments that govern the use of singular terms are made explicit as the contents of assertional commitments, they take the form of identity claims. Identity locutions permit the expression of claims that have the significance of intersubstitution licenses. Weakening inferences, the one-way inferential involvements that collectively constitute the asymmetric substitutional significance of the occurrence of predicate expressions, are made assertionally explicit by the use of quantified conditionals. Thus, "Benjamin Franklin is (=) the inventor of bifocals" and "Anything that walks, moves."

3. Simple Material Substitution-Inferential Commitments

The substitution inference from "The inventor of bifocals wrote about electricity" to "The first postmaster general of the United States wrote about electricity" is a material inference. Part of my associating the material content I do with the term "the inventor of bifocals" consists in the commitment I undertake to the goodness of the substitution inferences that correspond to replacements of occurrences of that term by occurrences of "the first postmaster general of the United States" (and vice versa). That commitment has a general substitution-inferential significance, which is to say that the particular material inference endorsed above is correct as an instance of a general pattern. That same material substitutional commitment regarding "the inventor of bifocals" and "the first postmaster general of the United States" governs also the propriety of the inference from "The inventor of bifocals was a printer" to "The first postmaster general of the United States was a printer," also that from "The inventor of bifocals spoke French" to "The first postmaster general of the United States spoke French," as well as a myriad of others. So one simple material substitution-inferential commitment regarding two expressions determines the correctness of a great many substitution inferences materially involving those expressions, across a great variety of substituted-in sentences and residual sentence frames.

Also, the substitution inferences to and from "The inventor of bifocals was a printer" are determined by all the simple material substitution-inferential commitments (SMSICs) that link the expression "the inventor of bifocals" with another. Nevertheless, not all occurrences of those expressions have their substitution-inferential significances determined in this way. For instance, it does not settle the propriety of the substitution inference from

The current postmaster general of the United States believes that the first postmaster general of the United States was a printer

to

The current postmaster general of the United States believes that the inventor of bifocals was a printer.[17]

These observations motivate the discrimination of certain occurrences of an expression, in a syntactic sense of 'occurrence', as in addition semantically significant occurrences of it. A subsentential expression has a syntactic occurrence as a component of (is exhibited by) a sentence just in case it is replaceable by other expressions of its category (either in the original sense of being substituted for or in the secondhand sense appropriate to expressions of substitutionally derived categories), saving sentencehood. (Syntactic categories are interreplaceability equivalence classes, since replacement is reversible and preservation of sentencehood symmetric.) For an occurrence of an expression in this syntactic sense to count also as having primary substitution-semantic occurrence in a sentence, the substitution inferences to and from that sentence, in which that expression is materially involved, must be governed (their proprieties determined) by the set of simple material substitution-inferential commitments that link that expression with another.[18]

How do SMSICs relating subsentential expressions settle the correctness of the substitution inferences in which the sentences exhibiting primary substitution-semantic occurrences of those expressions figure as premises and conclusions? According to a general pattern. A material substitution-inferential commitment regarding A and A' is a commitment to the effect that for any B such that AB is a sentence in which A has primary substitution-semantic occurrence, the inference from AB to $A'B$ is good. Likewise, a material substitution-inferential commitment regarding B and B' is a commitment to the effect that for any A such that AB is a sentence in which B has primary substitution-semantic occurrence, the inference from AB to AB' is good. Five points may be noted concerning this structure relating substitutional commitments to substitutional inferences.

First, *all* of the substitution inferences in which a sentence such as AB figures as premise or as conclusion are determined according to this pattern by all of the SMSICs dealing with expressions having primary substitution-semantic occurrences in AB (which might, but need not, be just A and B). Second, responsibility for those proprieties of substitution inferences to and from a sentence is apportioned between the various subsentential expressions having primary occurrences in it, with the SMSICs dealing with a particular expression responsible for the inferences in which that expression is materially involved. The content (determiner of material proprieties of inference) of each expression is represented by the set of SMSICs that relate it to other expressions. Only the collaboration of all of the SMSICs corresponding to subsentential expressions having primary occurrence in a sentence settles the correctness of the whole set of substitution inferences it appears in as premise or conclusion. Third, a consequence of this division of labor in the determination of the correctness of material inferences (assigning aspects of it to different sorts of expression) is that material inferential roles are determined thereby for novel compounds of familiar components. So even if no one has ever encountered the sentence $A'B'$, the SMSICs cited above determine a commitment to the propriety of the inference from AB to $A'B'$. Other SMSICs already in place may in the same way license the inference from $A'B'$ to $A''B'$, and so on. Accumulating the content (what determines material proprieties of inference) to be associated with subsentential expressions in the form of substitutional commitments regarding pairs of expressions, then, permits the projection of material proprieties of substitution inference involving a potentially large set of novel sentences from the proprieties involving relatively few familiar ones. Fourth, on this model it is clear how to understand additions to or alterations of content. For when I discover or decide (what would be expressed explicitly in the claim) that the inventor of bifocals is the inventor of lightning rods, and thereby undertake a new simple material substitution-inferential commitment, the substitution-inferential potentials both of sentences in which these expressions have primary occurrence and of others substitutionally linked to them are altered in determinate and predictable ways. Fifth, for the same reason, it is easy to understand what is involved in introducing new subsentential vocabulary as expressing novel contents. Such vocabulary will make exactly the same sort of contribution to the strictly inferential contents of sentences that the old vocabulary does, as soon as its use has been tied to that of the old vocabulary by suitable SMSICs.

The criteria of adequacy responded to by these five observations jointly constitute the *point* of discerning semantically significant subsentential structure, once the pragmatic, and so semantic, priority of sentences is acknowledged. Against the background of this sort of understanding of the semantically significant decomposition of sentences into their components, the formal difference between the material substitutional commitments governing singular terms and those governing predicates becomes particularly striking. The SMSICs that determine the material inferential significance of the occurrence of singular terms are symmetrical: a commitment to the correctness of the inference that results from substituting A' for A is also a commitment to the correctness of the inference that results from substituting A for A'. The set of SMSICs that determine the material inferential significance of the occurrence of any predicate, by contrast, include asymmetric ones. From this point of view, what is special about singular terms is that the simple material substitution-inferential commitments relating pairs of terms partition the set of terms into equivalence classes. This is what it is for it to be (particular) objects that singular terms purport to refer to. An equivalence class of inter-substitutable terms stands for an object. It follows from the substitutional definition of the object-specifying equivalence classes of terms that it makes no sense to talk of languages in which there is just one singular term (*pace* 'the Absolute' as Bradley and Royce tried to use that expression), nor of objects that can in principle be referred to in only one way (by one term). The SMSICs that confer material inferential content on predicates, by contrast, do not segregate those expressions into equivalence classes, and so do not confer a content that purports to pick out an object. The asymmetric structure conferred on the material contents of predicates is quite different.

There are, then, two fundamental sorts of substitution-inferential significance that the occurrence of expressions of various subsentential categories might have: symmetric and asymmetric. The claim so far is that it is a necessary condition for identifying some subsentential expression kind as a predicate that expressions of that kind be materially involved in some asymmetric substitution inferences, while it is a necessary condition for identifying some subsentential expression kind as a singular term that expressions of that kind be materially involved only in symmetric substitution inferences. These paired necessary semantic conditions distinguishing singular terms from predicates in terms of substitution-inferential significance (SIS) may be laid alongside the paired necessary syntactic conditions distinguishing singular terms from predicates in terms of substitution-structural role (SSR). The suggestion then is that these individually necessary conditions, symmetric SIS and substituted-for SSR, are jointly sufficient to characterize the use of a kind of expression that distinguishes it as playing the role of singular terms. In the rest of this chapter the expression 'singular term' is used to signify expressions that play this dual syntactic and semantic substitutional role. It is to whatever expressions play this role that the argument is addressed.

III. Why Are There Singular Terms?

1. Four Alternative Subsentential Analyses

Here is an answer to the question "What are singular terms?": they are expressions that are substituted for, and whose occurrence is symmetrically inferentially significant. The question "Why are there any singular terms?" can now be put more sharply: Why should the expressions that are substituted for be restricted to symmetric inferential significance? What function does this arrangement serve?

It is clear enough why the use of a substitutional scalpel to dissect sentential contents into subsentential components requires distinguishing expressions substituted for from substitutional frames. But why should any sort of subsentential expression have a symmetric SIS? And if some sort for some reason must, why should it be what is substituted for rather than the corresponding substitutional frames?

What are the alternatives? They are structured by the previous pair of distinctions, between two sorts of substitution-structural syntactic role and between two sorts of substitution-inferential semantic significance. So the possibilities are:

1. substituted *for* is symmetric;   substitutional *frame* is symmetric
2. substituted *for* is *a*symmetric;   substitutional *frame* is symmetric
3. substituted *for* is *a*symmetric;   substitutional *frame* is *a*symmetric
4. substituted *for* is symmetric;   substitutional *frame* is *a*symmetric

The final arrangement (4) is the one actualized in languages with singular terms. One way to ask why this combination of syntactic and semantic roles is favored is to ask what is wrong with the other ones. What rules out the combinations (1), (2), and (3)? What sort of consideration could? The strategy pursued here is to look at the constraints on the expressive power of a language that are imposed by each of those varieties of complex substitutional roles.

The first alternative is a good place to begin, for it is fairly easily eliminated from contention. The semantic point of discerning subsentential structure substitutionally is to codify an antecedent field of inferential proprieties concerning sentences by associating material contents with recombinable subsentential expressions so as to be able to derive those proprieties of inference, and to project further ones, according to a general pattern of substitution-inferential significance of material substitutional commitments. But the substituted-in sentences whose inferences are to be codified themselves stand in "one-way inferential involvements." The goodness of an inference may require that when the conclusion is substituted for the premise(s), some status (doxastic or assertional commitment, truth, and so on) is preserved. But the converse replacement need not preserve that status. Substitution inferences are not always reversible, saving correctness. Conclusions are often inferentially weaker than the premises from which they are inferred. A restriction to sentential contents conferrable by exclusively symmetrically valid material inferences is a restriction to sentential contents completely unrecognizable as such by us. But if both substituted-for expressions and the substitutional frames that are the patterns according to which they assimilate substituted-in sentences are significant only according to symmetric SMSICs, then asymmetric inferential relations involving substituted-in sentences can never be codified as substitution inferences materially involving subsentential expressions, and so licensed by the SMSICs regarding those expressions. Since the inferences to be codified include asymmetric ones, either the substituted-for expressions or the substitutional frames, or both, must be assigned asymmetric substitution-inferential significance.

The other two alternatives, (2) and (3), are alike in assigning the substituted-for expressions asymmetric substitution-inferential significance. If a good reason can be found for ruling out this combination of syntactic and semantic substitutional roles, then the employment of singular terms and their corresponding sentence frames will have been shown to be necessary. For if it can be shown that what is substituted for must have symmetric substitution-inferential significance, then since by the argument just offered the expressions playing some substitution-structural role must be asymmetric, it will follow that the substitution frames must permit asymmetric substitution. And this is just the combination of roles that has been put forward as characteristic of singular terms and predicates.

The first task was to answer the question "What are singular terms?" The answer that has emerged is that they are expressions that on the syntactic side play the substitution-structural role of being substituted for, and on the semantic side have symmetric substitution-inferential significances. The second task is to answer the question "Why are there any singular terms?" by presenting an explanation of why the inferential significance of the occurrence of expressions that are substituted for must be symmetric (and so segregate expressions materially into equivalence classes whose elements accordingly jointly purport to specify some one object). It takes the form of an argument that certain crucial sorts of expressive power would be lost in a language in which the significance of substituted-for expressions were permitted to be asymmetric.

2. The Argument

What is wrong with substituted-for expressions having asymmetric inferential significances? An asymmetric simple material substitution-inferential commitment linking substituted-for expressions *a* and *b* is a commitment to the goodness of all the inferences that are instances of a certain pattern. Where *Pa* is any sentence in which *a* has primary occurrence, the inference from *Pa* to *Pb* (the result of substituting *b* for *a* in *Pa*) is a good one, though perhaps its converse is not. The point of discerning primary occurrences of substituted-for expressions depends on these generalizations. For they provide the link that permits the projection of proprieties of substitution inference, based on associating particular substituted-fors with material contents in the form of determinate sets of simple substitution-inferential commitments relating their use to that of other substituted-fors. Whether the generalizations that animate asymmetrically significant substitutional commitments regarding substituted-fors make sense or not depends on the contents expressed by the sentences substituted in, and it is this fact that in the end turns out to mandate symmetric substitutional significances for what is substituted for.

In order to see how one might argue against admitting asymmetrically significant substituted-for expressions, consider what happens if there is a general recipe for producing, given any frame $Q\alpha$, a frame $Q'\alpha$ that is inferentially complementary to it, in the sense that each $Q'\alpha$ is to be so constructed that whenever the inference from Qx to Qy is good, but not vice versa (intuitively, because *y* is inferentially weaker than *x*, the way 'mammal' is inferentially weaker than 'dog'), the inference from $Q'y$ to $Q'x$ is good, but not vice versa, for any substituted-for expressions *x* and *y*. Such a situation precludes discerning *any* primary substitution-semantic occurrences of any substituted-for expressions. There would then be no syntactic occurrences of any substituted-for expressions whose substitution-inferential significance is correctly captured by an asymmetric SMSIC (the symmetric ones are not currently at issue). For an asymmetric substitution-inferential commitment relating *a* to *b* governs inferential proprieties via the generalization that for *any* frame $P\alpha$, the inference from *Pa* to *Pb* is a good one, though not in general the converse.

Under the hypothesis being considered, no matter what particular instance $P\alpha$ is chosen, it is possible to construct or choose a complementary predicate, $P'\alpha$, for which only the complementary pattern of substitution-inferential proprieties obtains. In the presence of a recipe for producing for arbitrary substitution frames other frames that are inferentially complementary to them, then, no proprieties of substitution inference can be captured by asymmetric SMSICs, and so no primary substitution-semantic occurrences of substituted-for expressions corresponding to them. The upshot of this line of thought, then, is that the existence of asymmetrically significant substituted-for expressions is incompatible with the presence in the language of expressive resources sufficient to produce, for arbitrary sentence frames, inferentially complementary ones. To explain why substituted-for subsentential expressions have symmetric substitution-inferential significances, which on the current understanding is to explain why there are singular terms, then, it will suffice to explain what sort of expressive impoverishment a language is condemned to if it eschews the locutions that would permit the general formation of inferentially complementary sentence frames.

When it has been seen that the particular constellation of syntactic and semantic roles characteristic of singular terms is necessitated by the presence in the language of vocabulary meeting this condition, it becomes urgent to see what locutions make possible the production of arbitrary inferentially complementary frames, and how dispensable the role they play in linguistic practice might be. What locutions have this power? Examples are not far to seek. The one to focus on is the *conditional*. Because conditionals make inferential commitments explicit as the contents of assertional commitments, inferentially weakening the antecedent of a conditional inferentially strengthens the conditional. Endorsing all the inferences from sentences exhibiting the frame "α is a dog" to the corresponding "α is a mammal" does not involve commitment to the goodness of the inferences from sentences exhibiting the frame "If α is a dog, α then belongs to an anciently domesticated species," to those exhibiting the frame "If α is a mammal, then α belongs to an anciently domesticated species." Instances of the first conditional are true claims expressing correct inferences, while instances of its substitution variant are false conditionals expressing incorrect inferences. Quite generally, let Qa be a particular sentence in which the substituted-for expression a has primary occurrence, and Qb be a substitutional variant of it, and let r be some other sentence. Then $Qa{\rightarrow}r$ is a sentence in which a has primary occurrence, and the symbol $Q'α$ may be introduced for the sentence frame associated with its occurrence, with the conditional above written as $Q'a$. If a is inferentially stronger than b, asymmetrically, then the inference from Qa to Qb is good, but not its converse (Thera is a dog, so Thera is a mammal).[19] But if that is so, then the inference from $Q'a$ to $Q'b$ cannot be good, for inferentially weakening the antecedent of a conditional inferentially strengthens the conditional.

This last formulation suggests another example. Inferentially weakening a claim inside a negation inferentially strengthens the compound negation. If the substitution inference from Qa to Qb is good but the converse not, then the substitution inference from $~Qa$ to $~Qb$ cannot be good. Embedding as a negated component, like embedding as the antecedent of a conditional, reverses inferential polarities. The conclusion is that any language containing a conditional or negation thereby has the expressive resources to formulate, given any sentence frame, a sentence frame that behaves inferentially in a complementary fashion, thereby ruling out the generalizations that would correspond to asymmetric simple material substitution-inferential commitments governing the expressions that are substituted for in producing such frames.

3. The Importance of Logical Sentential Operators

The conditional and negation are fundamental bits of *logical* vocabulary. Is it just a coincidence that it is logical sentence-compounding locutions that permit the systematic formation of inferentially inverting sentential contexts? The sentence q is inferentially weaker than the sentence p just in case everything that is a consequence of q is a consequence of p, but not vice versa (consequences are not preserved but pruned). It is an immediate consequence of this definition that inferentially weakening the premises of an inference can turn good inferences into bad ones. The defining job of the conditional is to codify inferences as claims (make it possible to express inferential commitments explicitly in the form of assertional commitments). It is essential to doing that job that embedded sentences that can play the role of premises and conclusions of inferences appear as components, antecedents and consequents, in the conditional. The contexts in which component sentences occur as antecedents accordingly must be inferentially inverting. Notice that this argument presupposes very little about the details of the use of the conditional involved. It is enough, for instance, if the conditional has the designated (semantic or pragmatic) status in case the inference it expresses preserves the designated status. As the defining job of the conditional is to codify inferences, that of negation is to codify incompatibilities. The negation of a claim is its inferentially minimal incompatible: $\sim p$ is what is entailed by everything materially incompatible with p.[20] These underlying incompatibilities induce a notion of inferential weakening: "Thera is a dog" incompatibility-entails, and so is inferentially stronger than, "Thera is a mammal," because everything incompatible with "Thera is a mammal" is incompatible with "Thera is a dog," but not vice versa (incompatibilities pruned, not preserved). It follows that incompatibility-inferentially weakening a negated claim incompatibility-inferentially strengthens the negation. "It is not the case that Thera is a mammal" is incompatibility-inferentially stronger than "It is not the case that Thera is a dog," just because "Thera is a mammal" is incompatibility-inferentially weaker than "Thera is a dog." Thus negation also enables the formation of arbitrary inferential complements. I argued in Chapter 1 that what makes both conditionals and negation, so understood, specifically logical vocabulary is that the material inferences and material inference-inducing incompatibilities of which they permit the assertionally explicit expression play a central role in conferring material contents on prelogical sentences. It is a direct result of this defining semantically expressive function that they form semantically inverting contexts.

Since it is the availability of such contexts that rules out asymmetrically significant substituted-for expressions, it follows that a language can have either the expressive power that goes with logical vocabulary or asymmetrically substitution-inferentially significant substituted-for expressions, but not both. It is leaving room for the possibility of logical locutions that enforces the discrimination of singular terms (and, as a consequence, of predicates) rather than some other sorts of subsentential expression.

Notice that the only logical locutions required for that argument are those whose roles are definable solely in terms of the behavior of *sentences*, before any sort of subsentential substitutional analysis has been undertaken. The argument does not depend on any particular features of the sentential contents that are available to begin with, which determine the proprieties of material inference that provide the targets for substitutional codification in (implicit or explicit) SMSICs. All that matters is the availability of the expressive power of logical sentential connectives.

But having to do without logical expressions would impoverish linguistic practice in fundamental ways. The use of any contentful sentence involves implicit commitment to the (material) correctness of the inference from the circumstances of appropriate application associated with that sentence to the consequences of such application. Introducing conditionals into a language permits these implicit, content-conferring, material-inferential commitments to be made explicit in the form of assertional commitments. This is important at the basic, purely sentential level of analysis for the same reason it becomes important later at the subsentential level, when identity and quantificational locutions can be introduced to make explicit the SMSICs that confer distinguishable material-inferential content on subsentential expressions. In each case, once made explicit in the form of claims, those content-conferring commitments are brought into the game of giving and asking for reasons. They become subject to explicit objection, for instance, by confrontation with materially incompatible assertions, and equally to explicit justification, for instance, by citation of materially sufficient inferential grounds. The task of forming and nurturing the concepts we talk and think with is brought out of the dim twilight of what remains implicit in unquestioned practice into the daylight of what becomes explicit as controversial principle. Material contents, once made explicit, can be shaped collectively, as interlocutors in different situations, physically and doxastically, but in concert with their fellows, provide objections and evidence, claims and counterclaims, and explore possible consequences and ways of becoming entitled to assert them. Logic is the linguistic organ of semantic self-consciousness and self-control. The expressive resources provided by logical vocabulary make it possible to criticize, control, and improve our concepts. To give this up is to give up a lot.[21] Yet, it has been argued, it is a direct (if unobvious) consequence of leaving open the possibility of introducing such inferentially explicitating vocabulary that the subsentential expressions that are substituted for will be singular terms, and their corresponding sentence frames will be predicates, as judged by the symmetric and asymmetric forms of their respective substitution-inferential significances.[22]

IV. Conclusion

The title of this chapter asks the double question "What are singular terms, and why are there any?" The strategy of the answer offered to the first query is to focus on substitution. The fundamental unit of language is the sentence, since it is by uttering freestanding sentences that speech acts are performed. Thus sentences are fundamental in the sense that it is coherent to interpret a community as using (its practices conferring content on) sentences but not subsentential expressions, while it is not coherent to interpret any community as using subsentential expressions but not sentences. But in fact there are good reasons why any community that uses sentences should also be expected to use subsentential expressions, indeed, subsentential expressions of particular kinds.

The notion of substitution provides a route from the discrimination of the fundamental sentential expressions to the discrimination of essentially subsentential expressions. To carve up sentences substitutionally is to assimilate them accordingly as occurrences of the same subsentential expressions are discerned in them. Such a decomposition is accomplished by a set of substitution transformations. The functional significance of discerning in a sentence an occurrence of one out of a set of expressions that can be substituted for is to treat the sentence as subject to a certain subclass of substitution transformations relating it to other, variant sentences. So the expressions that are substituting and substituted for can be used to index the transformations.[23] Two sentences are taken to exhibit the same substitutional sentence frame in case they are substitutional variants of each other, that is, are accessible one from the other by substitution transformations. These substitutional assimilations define two basic substitution-structural roles that essentially subsentential expression kinds could play. The first half of the answer to the first question "What are singular terms?" is then that *syntactically,* singular terms play the substitution-structural role of being substituted *for,* while predicates play the substitution-structural role of sentence frames.

The second half of the answer to that question is that *semantically,* singular terms are distinguished by their *symmetric* substitution-inferential significance. Thus, if a particular substitution transformation that corresponds to substituting one singular term for another preserves some semantically relevant sentential status (commitment, entitlement, truth, or whatever) when only primary occurrences are involved, no matter what the sentence frame, then the inverse transformation also preserves that status, regardless of frame. By contrast, every sentence frame is involved in weakening inferences, where there is some other frame such that replacing primary occurrences of the first by the second always preserves the relevant sentential status, no matter what structure of substituted-for expressions is exhibited, while the converse replacement is not always status-preserving. Because the simple material substitution-inferential commitments that articulate the semantic content associated with singular terms are symmetric, their transitive closure partitions the set of singular terms into equivalence classes of intersubstitutable substituted-for expressions. It is in virtue of this defining character of their use that singular terms can be said to "purport to refer to just one object."

The full answer to the question "What are singular terms?" is then that singular terms are substitutionally discriminated, essentially subsentential expressions that play a dual role. Syntactically they play the substitution-structural role of being substituted *for*. Semantically their primary occurrences have a *symmetric* substitution-inferential significance. Predicates, by contrast, are syntactically substitution-structural *frames,* and semantically their primary occurrences have an *asymmetric* substitution-inferential significance. This precise substitutional answer to the first question supplies a definite sense to the second one.

To ask why there are singular terms is to ask why expressions that are substituted for (and so of the basic substitution-structural kind) should have their significance governed by symmetric commitments, while sentence frames (expressions of the derivative substitution-structural kind) should have their significance governed in addition by asymmetric commitments. The strategy pursued in answer to this question is to focus on the use of logical vocabulary to permit the explicit *expression*, as the content of sentences, of relations among sentences that are partly constitutive of their being contentful. To say that subsentential expressions are used by a community as substituted-fors and substitution-structural frames is to say that the contents conferred by the practices of the community on the sentences in which those expressions have primary occurrence are related systematically to one another in such a way that they can be exhibited as the products of contents associated with the subsentential expressions, according to a standard substitutional structure. The problem of why there are singular terms arises because that structure need not, for all that has just been said, assume the specific form that defines singular terms and predicates.

But suppose the condition is added that the sentences whose proper use must be codifiable in terms of the proper use of their subsentential components is to include (or be capable of being extended so as to include) not only logically atomic sentences, but also sentences formed using the fundamental sentential logical vocabulary, paradigmatically conditionals and negation. This condition turns out to interact in intricate ways with the possibility of substitutional codification of sentential contents by subsentential ones—ways that when followed out can be seen to require just the combination of syntactic and semantic substitutional roles characteristic of singular terms and predicates. So the answer offered is that the existence of singular terms (and so of their complementary predicates) is the result of a dual expressive necessity. On the one hand, the material-inferential and material-incompatibility commitments regarding sentences must be implicitly substitutionally codifiable in terms of material-inferential and material-incompatibility commitments regarding the subsentential expressions that can be discerned within them or into which they can be analyzed, if the contents of novel sentences are to be projectable. On the other hand, those same commitments regarding sentences must be explicitly logically codifiable as the contents of assertional commitments, if the contents of nonlogical (as well as logical) sentences are to be available for public inspection, debate, and attempts at improvement. It is these two expressive demands, each intelligible entirely in terms of considerations arising already at the sentential level, that jointly give rise to the structure of symmetrically significant substituted-fors and asymmetrically significant substitution-structural sentence frames that defines the functional roles of singular terms and predicates.

This argument may be called an *expressive deduction* of the necessity of basic subsentential structure taking the form of terms and predicates. A language must be taken to have expressions functioning as singular terms if essentially subsentential structure is (substitutionally) discerned in it at all, and the language is expressively rich enough to contain fundamental sentential logical locutions—paradigmatically conditionals—which permit the assertionally explicit expression of material-inferential relations among nonlogical sentences, and negations, which permit the assertionally explicit expression of material-incompatibility relations among nonlogical sentences.

Logical vocabulary has the expressive role of making *explicit,* in the form of logically compound assertible sentential contents, the *implicit* material commitments in virtue of which logically atomic sentences have the contents that they do. Logic transforms semantic practices into principles. By providing the expressive tools permitting us to endorse in what we say what before we could endorse only in what we did, logic makes it possible for the development of the concepts by which we conceive our world and our plans (and so ourselves) to rise in part above the indistinct realm of mere tradition, of evolution according to the results of the thoughtless jostling of the habitual and the fortuitous, and enter the comparatively well lit discursive marketplace, where reasons are sought and proffered, and every endorsement is liable to being put on the scales and found wanting. The expressive deduction argues that subsentential structure takes the specific form of singular terms and predicates because only in that way can the full expressive benefits of substitutional subsentential analysis—codifying material correctnesses implicit in the use of sentences in material correctnesses implicit in the use of subsentential expressions—be combined with those afforded by the presence of full-blooded logical vocabulary of various sorts, performing its task of making explicit in claims what is implicit in the practical application of concepts.

In other words, languages have singular terms rather than some other kind of expression so that logic can help us talk and think in those languages about what we are doing, and why, when we talk and think in those languages. The full play of expressive power of even purely sentential logical vocabulary turns out to be incompatible with every sort of substitutional subsentential analysis save that in which essentially subsentential expressions playing the substitution-structural role of being substituted for have symmetric substitution-inferential significances, and those playing the substitution-structural role of sentence frames have asymmetric substitution-inferential significances. For to play its inference-explicitating role, the conditional, for instance, must form compound sentences whose antecedent substitution position is inferentially inverting. Only symmetrically significant expressions can be substituted for, and so form sentence frames, in such a context. That is why in languages with conditionals, subsentential structure takes the form of singular terms and predicates.

At the beginning of this chapter I pointed out that the principle that singular terms are used to talk about particular objects can be exploited according to two complementary directions of explanation. One might try to give an account of what particulars are, without using the concept *singular term,* and then proceed to define what it is to use an expression as a singular term by appeal to the relation of such terms to particulars. Or one might try to give an account of what singular terms are without using the concept *particular*, and then proceed to define what it is for something to be a particular by appeal to the relations of particulars to expressions used as terms. (It should of course be admitted that in either case the talking about relation will require substantial explanation, though that explanation may have to look quite different depending on which explanatory strategy it is conceived as abetting.) The answer presented here to the question "What are singular terms?" does not appeal to the concept of objects. So it provides just the sort of account required by the first stage of the second, Kant-Frege strategy for explaining the concept of objects.

It is worth pointing out that in the context of this order of explanation, to explain why there are singular terms is in an important sense to explain why there are objects—not why there is something (to talk about) rather than nothing (at all), but rather why what we talk about comes structured as propertied and related objects: "The limits of language (of that language which alone I understand) means the limits of my world."[24] To ask the question "Why are there singular terms?" is one way of asking the question "Why are there objects?" How odd and marvelous that the answer to both should turn out to be: Because it is so important to have something that means what *conditionals* mean!

FIVE

◆ ◆ ◆

A Social Route from Reasoning to Representing

I. Background

1. Thinking and Thinking About

One useful way of dividing up the broadly cognitive capacities that constitute our mindedness is to distinguish between our sentience and our sapience. Sentience is what we share with nonverbal animals such as cats—the capacity to be *aware* in the sense of being *awake*. Sentience, which so far as our understanding yet reaches is an exclusively biological phenomenon, is in turn to be distinguished from the mere reliable differential responsiveness we sentients share with artifacts such as thermostats and land mines. Sapience, by contrast, concerns *understanding* or intelligence rather than irritability or arousal. One is treating something as sapient insofar as one explains its behavior by attributing to it intentional states such as belief and desire as constituting *reasons* for that behavior. Sapients act as though reasons matter to them. They are rational agents in the sense that their behavior can be made intelligible, at least sometimes, by attributing to them the capacity to make practical inferences concerning how to get what they want, and theoretical inferences concerning what follows from what.

Besides thinking of sapience in terms of reasons and inference, it is natural to think of it in terms of truth. Sapients are believers, and believing is taking-true. Sapients are agents, and acting is making-true. To be sapient is to have states such as belief, desire, and intention, which are contentful in the sense that the question can appropriately be raised under what circumstances what is believed, desired, or intended would be *true*. Understanding such a content is grasping the conditions that are necessary and sufficient for its truth.

These two ways of conceiving sapience, in terms of inference and in terms of truth, have as their common explanatory target contents distinguished as intelligible by their *propositional* form. What we can offer as a reason, what we can take or make true, has a propositional content, a content of the sort that we express by the use of declarative sentences and ascribe by the use of 'that' clauses. Propositional contents stand in inferential relations, and they have truth conditions.

Whether we think of propositional content in terms of truth or in terms of reasons, we are still obliged to discuss also aboutness and representation. When we try to understand the thought or discourse of others, the task can be divided initially into two parts: understanding what they are thinking or talking about and understanding what they are thinking or saying about it. My primary aim here is to present a view of the relation between what is *said* or *thought* and what it is said or thought *about*. The former is the propositional dimension of thought and talk, and the latter is its *representational* dimension. The question I address is why any state or utterance that has propositional content also should be understood as having representational content. (For this so much as to be a question, it must be possible to characterize propositional content in nonrepresentational terms.)

The answer I defend is that the representational dimension of propositional contents should be understood in terms of their *social* articulation—how a propositionally contentful belief or claim can have a different significance from the perspective of the individual believer or claimer, on the one hand, than it does from the perspective of one who attributes that belief or claim to the individual, on the other. The context within which concern with what is thought and talked *about* arises is the assessment of how the judgments of one individual can serve as reasons for another. The representational content of claims and the beliefs they express reflect the social dimension of the game of giving and asking for reasons.

2. Kant

It may be remarked at the outset that it will not do just to think of the representational dimension of semantic contentfulness according to a designational paradigm—that is, on the model of the relation between a name and what it is a name of. For that relation is a *semantic* relation only in virtue of what one can go on to *do* with what is picked out by the name—what one can then *say* about it. Merely picking out an object or a possible state of affairs is not enough. What about it? One must say something about the object, claim that the state of affairs obtains or is a fact.

One of Kant's epoch-making insights, confirmed and secured for us also by Frege and Wittgenstein, is his recognition of the *primacy of the propositional*. The pre-Kantian tradition took it for granted that the proper order of semantic explanation begins with a doctrine of concepts or terms, divided into singular and general, whose meaningfulness can be grasped independently of and prior to the meaningfulness of judgments. Appealing to this basic level of interpretation, a doctrine of judgments then explains the combination of concepts into judgments, and how the correctness of the resulting judgments depends on what is combined and how. Appealing to this derived interpretation of judgments, a doctrine of consequences finally explains the combination of judgments into inferences, and how the correctness of inferences depends on what is combined and how.

Kant rejects this. One of his cardinal innovations is the claim that the fundamental unit of awareness or cognition, the minimum graspable, is the *judgment*. Judgments are fundamental, since they are the minimal unit one can take *responsibility* for on the cognitive side, just as actions are the corresponding unit of responsibility on the practical side. (The Transcendental Unity of Apperception is a unity defined by an equivalence relation of *coresponsibility*. The "emptiest of all representations," the " 'I think' that can accompany all representations" expresses the formal dimension of responsibility *for* judgments. The "object = X," concern for which distinguishes transcendental from general logic, expresses the formal dimension of judgments' responsibility *to* something. Thus concepts can be understood only as abstractions, in terms of the role they play in judging. A concept just is a predicate of a possible judgment,[1] which is why *"The only use which the understanding can make of concepts is to form judgments by them."*[2] For Kant, any discussion of content must start with the contents of judgments, since anything else has content only insofar as it contributes to the contents of judgments. This is why his transcendental logic can investigate the presuppositions of contentfulness in terms of the categories, that is, the "functions of unity in judgment."[3] This explanatory strategy is taken over by Frege, for whom the semantic notion of conceptual content ultimately has the theoretical task of explaining pragmatic *force*—the paradigmatic variety of which is *assertional* force, which attaches only to declarative sentences. As the later Wittgenstein puts the point, only the utterance of a sentence makes a move in the language game. Applying a concept is to be understood in terms of making a claim or expressing a belief. The concept *concept* is not intelligibe apart from the possibility of such application in *judging*.

The lesson is that the relation between designation and what is designated can be understood only as an aspect of judging or claiming *that* something (expressed by a declarative sentence, not by a singular term or predicate by itself) is so, that is, is *true*. That is judging, believing, or claiming *that* a proposition or claim is true (expresses or states a fact), *that* something is *true of* an object or collection of objects, *that* a predicate is *true of* something else. Thus one must be concerned with what is said or expressed, as well as what it is said *of* or true *of*—the thought as well as what the thought is *about*.

3. Inference and Content

Accordingly we start our story with an approach to propositional contents: what can be *said* or *believed* or *thought*, in general, what can be *taken* (to be) *true*. The guiding idea is that the essential feature distinguishing what is propositionally contentful is that it can serve both as a premise and as the conclusion of *inferences*. Taking (to be) true is treating as a fit premise for inferences. This is exploiting Frege's semantic principle—that good inferences never lead from true premises to conclusions that are not true—not in order to define good inferences in terms of their preservation of truth, but rather to define truth as what is preserved by good inferences.

On the side of propositionally contentful *intentional states*, paradigmatically *belief*, the essential inferential articulation of the propositional is manifested in the form of intentional interpretation or explanation. Making behavior intelligible according to this model is taking the individual to act for *reasons*. This is what lies behind Dennett's slogan, "Rationality is the mother of intention." The role of belief in imputed pieces of practical reasoning, leading from beliefs and desires to the formation of intentions, is essential to intentional explanation—and so is reasoning in which both premise and conclusion have the form of believables.

On the side of propositionally contentful *speech acts*, paradigmatically assertion, the essential inferential articulation of the propositional is manifested in the fact that the core of specifically *linguistic* practice is the game of giving and asking for *reasons*. Claiming or asserting is what one must do in order to give a reason, and it is a speech act that reasons can be demanded for. Claims both serve as and stand in need of reasons or justifications. They have the contents they have in part in virtue of the role they play in a network of inferences.

Indeed, the *conceptual* should be distinguished precisely by its inferential articulation. This is a point on which traditional empiricism needed instruction by traditional rationalism. What is the difference between a parrot or a thermostat that represents a light as being red or a room as being cold by exercising its reliable differential responsive disposition to utter the noise "That's red" or to turn on the furnace, on the one hand, and a knower who does so by applying the concepts *red* and *cold*, on the other? What is the knower able to *do* that the parrot and the thermostat cannot? After all, they may respond differentially to *just* the same range of stimuli. The knower is able to *use* the differentially elicited response in *inference*. The knower has the practical know-how to situate that response in a network of inferential relations—to tell what follows from something being red or cold, what would be evidence for it, what would be incompatible with it, and so on. For the knower, taking something to be red or cold is making a move in the game of giving and asking for reasons—a move that can justify other moves, be justified by still other moves, and that closes off or precludes still further moves. The parrot and the thermostat lack the concepts in spite of their mastery of the corresponding noninferential differential responsive dispositions, precisely because they lack the practical mastery of the inferential articulation in which grasp of conceptual content consists.

The idea, then, is to start with a story about the sayable, thinkable, believable (and so propositional) contents expressed by the use of declarative sentences and 'that' clauses derived from them—a story couched in terms of their roles in *inference*.[4] Conceptual content is in the first instance *inferentially* articulated. To approach the representational dimension of semantic content from this direction, it is necessary to ask about the relation between *inference* and *reference*. This is to ask about the relation between what is said or thought and what it is said or thought *about*. How can the representational dimension of conceptual content be brought into the inferential picture or propositional contents? The thesis to be elaborated here is that the representational dimension of discourse reflects the fact that conceptual content is not only *inferentially* articulated but also *socially* articulated. The game of giving and asking for reasons is an essentially *social* practice.

4. The Normative Character of Concept Use

The rationale for such a claim emerges most clearly from consideration of certain very general features of discursive practice. Here it is useful to start with another of Kant's fundamental insights, into the *normative* character of the significance of what is conceptually contentful. His idea is that judgments and actions are above all things that we are *responsible* for. Kant understands concepts as having the form of *rules*, which is to say that they specify how something *ought* (according to the rule) to be done. The understanding, the conceptual faculty, is the faculty of grasping rules, of appreciating the distinction between correct and incorrect application they determine. Judgings and doings are acts that have contents that one can take or make true and for which the demand for reasons is in order. What is distinctive about them is the way they are governed by rules. Being in an intentional state or performing an intentional action has a normative significance. It counts as undertaking (acquiring) an obligation or commitment; the content of the commitment is determined by the rules that are the concepts in terms of which the act or state is articulated. Thus Kant picks us out as distinctively normative or rule-governed creatures.

Descartes inaugurated a new philosophical era by conceiving of what he took to be the ontological distinction between the mental and the physical in epistemological terms, in terms of accessibility to cognition, in terms, ultimately, of certainty. Kant launched a new philosophical epoch by shifting the center of concern from *certainty* to *necessity*. Whereas Descartes's descriptive conception of intentionality, centering on certainty, picks out as essential our grip on the concepts employed in cognition and action, Kant's normative conception of intentionality, centering on necessity, treats their grip on us as the heart of the matter. The attempt to understand the source, nature, and significance of the norms implicit in our concepts—both those that govern the theoretical employment of concepts in inquiry and knowledge and those that govern their practical employment in deliberation and action—stands at the very center of Kant's philosophical enterprise. The most urgent question for Kant is how to understand the *rulishness* of concepts, how to understand their *authority, bindingness,* or *validity*. It is this normative character that he calls *Notwendigkeit,* "necessity."

The lesson to be learned from this Kantian normative conceptual pragmatics is that judging and acting are distinguished from other doings by the kind of *commitment* they involve. Judging or claiming is staking a claim—undertaking a commitment. The conceptual articulation of these commitments, their status as distinctively *discursive* commitments, consists in the way they are liable to demands for *justification,* and the way they serve both to justify some further commitments and to preclude the justification of some other commitments. Their propositional contentfulness consists precisely in this inferential articulation of commitments and entitlements to those commitments.

Specifically *linguistic* practices are those in which some performances are accorded the significance of assertions or claimings—the undertaking of inferentially articulated (and so propositionally contentful) commitments.[5] Mastering such linguistic practices is a matter of learning how to keep score on the inferentially articulated commitments and entitlements of various interlocutors, oneself included. Understanding a speech act—grasping its discursive significance—is being able to attribute the right commitments in response. This is knowing how it changes the score of what the performer and the audience are committed and entitled to.

One way of thinking about the claims by which discursive commitments are expressed is in terms of the interaction of inferentially articulated *authority* and *responsibility*. In making an assertion, one lends to the asserted content one's *authority*, licensing others to undertake a corresponding commitment to use as a premise in *their* reasoning. Thus one essential aspect of this model of discursive practice is *communication:* the interpersonal, intracontent inheritance of entitlement to commitments. In making an assertion one also undertakes a *responsibility*—to justify the claim if appropriately challenged, and thereby to redeem one's entitlement to the commitment acknowledged by the claiming. Thus another essential aspect of this model of discursive practice is *justification:* the intrapersonal, intercontent inheritance of entitlement to commitments.

II. Analysis

1. Representation and Communication

One can pick out what is *propositionally* contentful to begin with as whatever can serve both as a premise and as a conclusion in *inference*—what can be offered as, and itself stand in need of, *reasons*. Understanding or grasping such a propositional content is a kind of know-how—practical mastery of the game of giving and asking for reasons, being able to tell what is a reason for what, distinguish good reasons from bad. To play such a game is to keep *score* on what various interlocutors are committed and entitled to. Understanding the content of a speech act or a belief is being able to accord the performance of that speech act or the acquisition of that belief the proper practical significance—knowing how it would change the score in various contexts. Semantic, that is to begin with, inferential, relations are to be understood in terms of this sort of pragmatic scorekeeping. Taking it that the claim expressed by one sentence entails the claim expressed by another is treating anyone who is committed to the first as thereby committed to the second. We typically think about inference solely in terms of the relation between premise and conclusion, that is, as a monological relation among propositional contents. Discursive practice, the giving and asking for reasons, however, involves both inter*content* and inter*personal* relations. The claim is that the representational aspect of the propositional contents that play the inferential roles of premise and conclusion should be understood in terms of the social or dialogical dimension of communicating reasons, of assessing the significance of reasons offered by others.

If whatever plays a suitable role in inference is propositionally contentful, and whatever is propositionally contentful therefore also has representational content, then nothing can deserve to count as specifically *inferential* practice unless it at least implicitly involves a representational dimension. Nonetheless, one can give sufficient conditions for a social practice to qualify as according *inferentially articulated* significances to performances, that is, to be a practice of making claims that can serve as reasons for others, and for which reasons can be demanded, without using any specifically representational vocabulary. That is what the model of discursive practice as keeping score on commitments and entitlements does. The story I want to tell, then, is how the implicit representational dimension of the inferential contents of claims arises out of the difference in social perspective between *producers* and *consumers* of reasons. The aim is an account in nonrepresentational terms of what is expressed by the use of explicitly representational vocabulary.

The connection between *representation,* on the one hand, and *communication* or the *social* dimension of inferential practice, on the other, is sufficiently unobvious that I want to start with two quick points that may help show why one could so much as think that representation could be understood in these terms. Consider a rational reconstruction of the dialectic that led Quine to displace *meaning* as the central semantic concept in favor of *reference,* in the wake of "Two Dogmas of Empiricism." Quine had taken it that meaning must at least determine inferential role. But what follows from endorsing a claim—what else that endorsement commits one to—depends on what concomitant commitments are available to serve as auxiliary hypotheses in extracting those inferential consequences. So the inferential significance of a belief depends on what else one believes. Thus the unit of meaning should be taken to be a whole theory, not just a single sentence. But this means that if two interlocutors have different beliefs, they mean different things by the sentences they utter. On this account it is not clear how the possibility of communication can be made intelligible as a matter of sharing meanings. But if attention is shifted instead to *reference,* the difficulty disappears. The Zoroastrian may *mean* something different by the word 'sun' than I do (it has a different meaning in her mouth than in my ear) because of the difference in her collateral commitments, but she can still be talking *about* the same thing, the sun. Equally significantly, though Rutherford may have meant something different by 'electron' than I do, we can still be understood as referring to the same things, electrons, and classifying them as falling in the same extension, that of subatomic particles. So talk of what one is talking *about* addresses worries that would otherwise be raised by theories of meaning with *holistic* consequences. More important in the current context, a concern with explaining the possibility of *communication* can lead to a concern with *reference* and *representation.* The second point in some ways reverses this order of approach.

The overall claim I am concerned with is that assessment of what people are talking and thinking *about,* rather than what they are saying about it, is a feature of the essentially *social* context of *communication.* Talk about representation is talk about what it is to secure communication by being able to use one another's judgments as reasons, as premises in our own inferences, even just hypothetically, to assess their significance in the context of our own collateral commitments. As one way to get a preliminary taste for how one could think that representational semantic talk could be understood as expressing differences in social perspective among interlocutors, consider how assessments of *truth* work. Perhaps the central context in which such assessments classically arise is attributions of *knowledge*. According to the traditional JTB account, knowledge is justified true belief. Transposed into a specification of a normative status something could be taken to have by interlocutors who are keeping score of one another's commitments and entitlements, this account requires that in order for it to be *knowledge* that a scorekeeper takes another to have, that scorekeeper must adopt three sorts of practical attitude. First, the scorekeeper must *attribute* an inferentially articulated, hence propositionally contentful, *commitment*. This corresponds to the *belief* condition on knowledge. Second, the scorekeeper must *attribute* a sort of inferential *entitlement* to that commitment. This corresponds to the *justification* condition on knowledge. What is it that then corresponds to the third, *truth* condition on knowledge? For the scorekeeper to take the attributed claim to be true is just for the scorekeeper to endorse that claim. That is, the third condition is that the scorekeeper himself *undertake* the same commitment attributed to the candidate knower.

Undertaking a commitment is adopting a certain *normative stance* with respect to a claim; it is not attributing a property to it. The classical metaphysics of truth properties misconstrues what one is doing in endorsing the claim as *describing* in a special way. It confuses *attributing* and *undertaking* or *acknowledging* commitments, the two fundamental social flavors of deontic practical attitudes that institute normative statuses. It does so by assimilating the third condition on treating someone as having knowledge to the first two. Properly understanding truth talk in fact requires understanding just this difference of social perspective: between *attributing* a normative status to another and *undertaking* or adopting it oneself.[6] It is the practice of assessing the truth of claims that underlies the idea that propositional contents can be understood in terms of truth conditions. What I want to do is to show how this idea of *truth* claims as expressing differences in social perspective can be extended to representation more generally.

2. *De dicto* and *De re*

The prime explicitly representational locution of natural languages is *de re ascriptions of propositional attitudes*. It is their use in these locutions that make the words 'of' and 'about' express the intentional directedness of thought and talk—their use in sentences such as

> "The time has come," the walrus said,
>> "To talk *of* many things:
> *Of* shoes—and ships—and sealing-wax—
>> *Of* cabbages—and kings—"

or

> The hunter's belief that there was a deer in front of her was actually a belief *about* a cow.

as distinct from their use in phrases such as "the pen of my aunt" and "weighing about five pounds." Thus, in order to identify vocabulary in alien languages that means what 'of' and 'about' used in this sense do, one must find expressions of *de re* ascriptions of propositional attitudes. It is these ascriptions that we use to *say* what we are talking and thinking *about*. My strategy here is to address the question of how to understand what is expressed by representational vocabulary by asking how expressions must be *used* in order to qualify as *de re* ascriptions of propositional attitudes.

What do they make explicit? What are we *doing* when we talk and think about what we are talking and thinking *about*? This is a strategy for trying to understand intentionality generally, from a pragmatist point of view.

The tradition distinguishes two readings of or senses that can be associated with propositional attitude ascriptions. Ascriptions *de dicto* attribute belief in a *dictum* or saying, while ascriptions *de re* attribute belief about some *res* or thing. The distinction arises with sentential operators other than 'believes'. Consider beginning with the claim:

The president of the United States will be black by the year 2020.

Read *de dicto*, this means that the dictum or sentence

The president of the United States is black.

will be true by the year 2020. Read *de re*, it means that the *res* or thing, the present president of the United States (namely, as I write, Bill Clinton) will be black by the year 2020. Our concern here is with how this distinction applies to ascriptions of propositional attitude—though it is a criterion of adequacy on the account offered here that it can be extended to deal with these other contexts as well. Clearly the difference has to do with *scope*, a way of expressing the difference between two different possible orders in which one can apply the operations of (a) determining who the definite description picks out, and (b) applying the temporal operator to move the time of evaluation of the whole sentence forward. Doing (a) first yields the *de re* reading, while doing (b) first yields the *de dicto* reading. I want to look a little deeper at the phenomenon.

In ordinary parlance the distinction between *de dicto* and *de re* readings is the source of systematic ambiguity. Sometimes, as in the case above, one of the readings involves a sufficiently implausible claim that it is easy to disambiguate. It is best, however, to regiment our usage slightly in order to mark the distinction explicitly. This can be done with little strain to our ears by using 'that' and 'of' in a systematic way. Consider:

> Henry Adams believed the inventor of the lightning rod did not invent the lightning rod.

It is quite unlikely that what is intended is the *de dicto*

> Henry Adams believed **that** the inventor of the lightning rod did not invent the lightning rod.

Adams would presumably not have endorsed the *dictum* that follows the 'that'. It is entirely possible, however, that the *de re* claim

> Henry Adams believed **of** the inventor of the lightning rod **that** he did not invent the lightning rod.

is true. For since the inventor of the lightning rod is the inventor of bifocals (namely, Benjamin Franklin), this latter claim could be true if Henry Adams had the belief that would be ascribed *de dicto* as

> Henry Adams believed **that** the inventor of bifocals did not invent the lightning rod.

(A proper Bostonian, loath to give such credit to someone from Philadelphia, Adams maintained that Franklin only popularized the lightning rod.)

Quine emphasizes that the key grammatical difference between these two sorts of ascriptions concerns the propriety of *substitution* for singular terms occurring in them. Expressions occurring in the *de re* portion of an ascription—within the scope of the 'of' operator in the regimented versions—have in his terminology *referentially transparent* uses: coreferential terms can be intersubstituted *salva veritate*, that is, without changing the truth value of the whole ascription. By contrast, such substitution in the *de dicto* portion of an ascription—within the scope of the 'that' operator in the regimented versions—may well change the truth value of the whole ascription. Syntactically, *de re* ascriptions may be thought of as formed from *de dicto* ones by *exporting* a singular term from within the 'that' clause, prefacing it with 'of', and putting a pronoun in the original position. Thus the *de dicto* form

S believes that $\phi(t)$

becomes the *de re*

S believes **of** *t* that $\phi(\text{it})$.

The significance of Quine's fundamental observation that the key difference between these two sorts of ascription lies in the circumstances under which the substitution of coreferential expressions is permitted was obscured by considerations that are from my point of view extraneous:

1. Quine's idiosyncratic view that singular terms are dispensable in favor of the quantificational expressions he takes to be the genuine locus of referential commitment leads him to look only at quantified ascriptions, embroils his discussion in issues of existential commitment, and diverts him into worries about when 'exportation' is legitimate.

2. This emphasis led in turn (Kaplan bears considerable responsibility here) to ignoring the analysis of ordinary *de re* ascriptions in favor of what I call *epistemically strong de re* ascriptions, which are used to attribute a privileged epistemic relation to the object talked or thought about. This detour had fruitful consequences for our appreciation of special features of the behavior of demonstratives (and, as a result, of proper name tokenings anaphorically dependent on them), particularly in modal contexts. But from the point of view of understanding aboutness in general—my topic here—it was a detour and a distraction nonetheless.

The important point is, as the regimentation reminds us, that it is *de re* propositional attitude-ascribing locutions that we use in everyday life to express what we are talking and thinking *of* or *about*. One way of trying to understand the representational dimension of propositional content is accordingly to ask what is expressed by this fundamental sort of representational locution. What are we *doing* when we make claims about what someone is talking or thinking *about*? How must vocabulary be used in order for it to deserve to count as expressing such *de re* ascriptions? Answering that question in a way that does not itself employ representational vocabulary in specifying that use is then a way of coming to understand representational relations in nonrepresentational terms.

3. Undertaking and Attributing

The rest of this chapter is about the expressive role of *de re* ascriptions. I present it in the technical vocabulary I prefer, which is in some ways idiosyncratic; but the basic point about the way in which the use of this paradigmatic representational locution expresses differences in social perspective does not depend on the details of that idiom.[7]

Recall that I think we should understand discursive practice in terms of the adoption of practical attitudes by which interlocutors keep score on one another's commitments (and entitlements to those commitments, but we can ignore them here). Claiming (and so, ultimately, judging) is *undertaking* or *acknowledging* a commitment that is propositionally contentful in virtue of its *inferential* articulation. The large task is to show what it is about that inferential articulation in virtue of which claimable contents are therefore also *representational* contents. This is to move from propositional contents introduced as potential premises and conclusions of inferences, via the social dimension of inferential articulation that consists of giving and asking for reasons of one another in communication, to propositions as talking of or about objects and saying of them how they are. (I give short shrift here to the *objectivity* part of the claim—it is the topic of the next chapter—

but think about how assessments of *truth* were presented above as distinct from assessments of *belief* and *justification*.)

Undertaking a commitment is doing something that makes it appropriate for others to *attribute* it. This can happen in two different ways. First, one may *acknowledge* the commitment, paradigmatically by being disposed to *avow* it by an overt assertion. Or one may acknowledge it by employing it as a premise in one's theoretical or practical reasoning. This latter includes being disposed to *act* on it *practically*—taking account of it as a premise in the practical reasoning that stands behind one's intentional actions. Second, one may undertake the commitment *consequentially*, that is, as a conclusion one is committed to as an inferential consequence entailed by what one *does* acknowledge. These correspond to two senses of 'believe' that are often not distinguished: the sense in which one believes only what one takes oneself to believe, and the sense in which one believes willy-nilly whatever one's beliefs commit one to. (The fact that people often move back and forth between belief in the empirical sense, which does not involve inferential closure, and belief in the logical or ideal sense, which does, is one of the reasons why when being careful I prefer to talk in terms of commitments rather than beliefs. I do not officially believe in beliefs.) The second sense is the one in which if I believe Kant revered Hamann, and I believe Hamann was the Magus of the North, then whether the question has ever arisen for me or not, whether I know it or not, I in fact believe Kant revered the Magus of the North, for I have committed myself to that claim.

Attributing beliefs or commitments is a practical attitude that is *implicit* in the scorekeeping practices within which alone anything can have the significance of a claim or a judgment. *Ascribing* beliefs or commitments is making that *implicit* practical attitude *explicit* in the form of a claim. In a language without explicit attitude-ascribing locutions such as the 'believes that' or 'claims that' operator, attributing commitments is something one can only *do*. Propositional attitude-ascribing locutions make it possible explicitly to *say* that that is what one is doing: to express that practical deontic scorekeeping attitude as a propositional content, that is, as the content of a claim. In this form it can appear as a premise or conclusion of an inference; it becomes something which can be offered as a reason, and for which reasons can be demanded. The paradigm of the genus of *explicitating* vocabulary, of which propositional attitude-ascribing locutions are a species, is the conditional. The use of conditionals makes explicit as the content of a claim, and so something one can *say*, the endorsement of an *inference*—an attitude one could otherwise manifest only by what one *does*. Ascriptional vocabulary such as 'believes' or 'claims' makes *attribution* of doxastic commitments explicit in the form of claimable contents.

4. Ascribing

In asserting an ascriptional claim of the form

S believes (or is committed to the claim) that $\phi(t)$,

one is accordingly doing two things, adopting two different sorts of deontic attitude: one is *attributing* one doxastic commitment, to $\phi(t)$, and one is *undertaking* another, namely, a commitment to the ascription. The explicitating role of ascriptional locutions means that the content of the commitment one *undertakes* is to be understood in terms of what one is doing in *attributing* the first commitment.

The ascription above specifies the content of the commitment attributed by using an unmodified 'that' clause, which according to our regimentation corresponds to an ascription *de dicto*. A full telling of my story requires that quite a bit be said about how these ascriptions work, but I am not going to do that here. Roughly, the ascriber who specifies the content of the attributed commitment in the *de dicto* way is committed to the target being prepared to *acknowledge* the attributed commitment in essentially the terms specified—that is, to endorse the *dictum*.[8]

I want to take an appropriate account of *de dicto* ascriptions of propositional attitudes for granted and show what is different about *de re* ascriptions, those that are regimented in the form:

S claims **of** *t* that ɸ(it).

I think that the beginning of wisdom in this area is the realization that (once what I have called 'epistemically strong *de re* ascriptions' have been put to one side) the distinction between *de dicto* and *de re* should be understood to distinguish not two kinds of *belief* or belief-contents, but two kinds of *ascription*—in particular, two different *styles* in which the *content* of the commitment ascribed can be *specified*.[9] (Dennett is perhaps the most prominent commentator who has taken this line.)[10]

In specifying the content of the claim that is attributed by an ascription, one finds that a question can arise as to who the ascriber takes to be responsible for this being a way of *saying* (that is, making explicit) what is believed—the content of the commitment. Consider the sly prosecutor who characterizes his opponent's claim by saying:

The defense attorney believes a pathological liar is a trustworthy witness.

We can imagine that the defense attorney hotly contests this characterization:

Not so; what I believe is that the man who just testified is a trustworthy witness.

To which the prosecutor might reply:

Exactly, and I have presented evidence that ought to convince anyone that the man who just testified is a pathological liar.

If the prosecutor were being fastidious in characterizing the other's claim, he would make it clear who is responsible for what: the defense attorney claims that a certain man is a trustworthy witness, and the prosecutor claims that that man is a pathological liar.

The disagreement is about whether this guy is a liar, not about whether liars make trustworthy witnesses. Using the regimentation suggested above, the way to make this explicit is with a *de re* specification of the content of the belief ascribed. What the prosecutor *ought* to say (matters of courtroom strategy aside) is:

> The defense attorney claims **of** a pathological liar that he is a trustworthy witness.

This way of putting things makes explicit the division of responsibility involved in the ascription. That someone is a trustworthy witness is part of the commitment that is *attributed* by the ascriber, that that individual is in fact a pathological liar is part of the commitment that is *undertaken* by the ascriber. (Think back to the account of the role of the truth condition in attributions of knowledge.) Certainly in thinking about these matters, *we* as theorists should use such a disambiguating regimentation, in keeping with the analytic credo expressing commitments to faith, hope, and clarity (even if we are not sure that the greatest of these is clarity).

Ascription always involves attributing one doxastic commitment and, since ascriptions are themselves claims or judgments, undertaking another. My suggestion is that the expressive function of *de re* ascriptions of propositional attitude is to make explicit which aspects of what is said express commitments that are being *attributed* and which express commitments that are *undertaken*. The part of the content specification that appears within the *de dicto* 'that' clause is limited to what, according to the ascriber, the one to whom the commitment is ascribed would (or in a strong sense should) *acknowledge* as an expression of what that individual is committed to. The part of the content specification that appears within the scope of the *de re* 'of' includes what, according to the *ascriber* of the commitment (but not necessarily according to the one to whom it is ascribed), is acknowledged as an expression of what the target of the ascription is committed to. (This is what the target should, according to the ascriber, acknowledge only in a much weaker sense of 'should'.) Thus the marking of portions of the content specification of a propositional attitude ascription into *de dicto* and *de re* portions makes explicit the essential deontic scorekeeping distinction of *social* perspective between commitments attributed and those undertaken.

5. Substitutional Commitments

The difference expressed by segregating the content specification of a propositional attitude ascription into distinct *de re* and *de dicto* regions, marked in our regimentation by 'of' and 'that', can be thought of in terms of *inferential* and *substitutional* commitments. According to the model I started with, propositional, that is, assertible, contents are inferentially articulated. Grasping such a content is being able to distinguish in practice what should follow from endorsing it, and what such endorsement should follow from. But the consequences of endorsing a given claim depends on what other commitments are available to be employed as auxiliary hypotheses in the inference. The ascriber of a doxastic commitment has two different perspectives available from which to draw those auxiliary hypotheses in specifying the content of the commitment being ascribed: that of the one to whom it is *ascribed* and that of the one *ascribing* it. Where the specification of the content depends only on auxiliary premises that (according to the ascriber) the target of the ascription *acknowledges* being committed to, though the ascriber may not, it is put in *de dicto* position, within the 'that' clause. Where the specification of the content depends on auxiliary premises that the *ascriber* endorses, but the target of the ascription may not, it is put in *de re* position.

   More particularly, the use of expressions as singular terms is governed by *substitution*-inferential commitments.[11] The rule for determining the scorekeeping significance and so the expressive function of *de re* ascriptions that I am proposing is then the following. Suppose that according to *A*'s scorekeeping on commitments, B acknowledges commitment to the claim $\phi(t)$. Then A can make this attribution of commitment explicit in the form of a claim by saying:

> B claims **that** $\phi(t)$.

If in addition A acknowledges commitment to the identity $t = t'$, then whether or not A takes it that B would acknowledge that commitment, A can also characterize the content of the commitment ascribed to B by saying:

> B claims **of** t' that ϕ(it).

Again, the question just is whose substitutional commitments one is permitted to appeal to in specifying the consequences someone is committed to by acknowledging a particular doxastic commitment. Where in characterizing the commitment the ascriber has exfoliated those consequences employing only commitments the ascriptional target would acknowledge, the content specification is *de dicto*. Where the ascriber has employed substitutional commitments he himself, but perhaps not the target, endorses, the content specification is *de re*.

The question might then naturally be asked, are there locutions that perform the converse function, permitting one to *undertake* an *assertional* commitment, while *attributing* to another responsibility for the use of the singular term that settles what *substitutional* commitments are to be used in extracting its inferential consequences? I think this important expressive role is played by *scare quotes*. Suppose a politician says:

> The patriotic freedom fighters liberated the village.

Disagreeing with the characterization, but wanting to stipulate that she is referring to the same folks, his opponent might respond:

> Those "patriotic freedom fighters" massacred the entire population.

Saying this is attributing responsibility for use of the term, while undertaking responsibility for the claim. I do not see why the expressive role of scare quotes is not every bit as philosophically significant as that of *de re* ascriptions, though the relative mass of the literature devoted to these two topics suggests that this is an idiosyncratic view.

Understood in the way I have suggested, what is expressed by *de re* specifications of the contents of the beliefs of others is crucial to *communication*. Being able to understand what others are saying, in the sense that makes their remarks available for use as premises in one's own inferences, depends precisely on being able to specify those contents in *de re*, and not merely *de dicto*, terms. If the only way I can specify the content of the shaman's belief is by a *de dicto* ascription:

> He believes malaria can be prevented by drinking the liquor distilled from the bark of that kind of tree,

I may not be in a position to assess the truth of his claim. It is otherwise if I can specify that content in the *de re* ascription

> He believes of quinine that malaria can be prevented by drinking it,

for 'quinine' is a term with rich inferential connections to others I know how to employ. If he says that the seventh god has just risen, I may not know what to make of his remark. Clearly he will take it to have consequences that I could not endorse, so nothing in my mouth could *mean* just what his remark does. But if I am told that the seventh god is the sun, then I can specify the content of his report in a more useful form:

> He claims of the sun that it has just risen,

which I can extract *information* from, that is, can use to generate premises that I can reason with. Again, suppose a student claims:

The largest number that is not the sum of the squares of distinct primes is the sum of at most twenty-seven primes.

He may have no idea what that number is, or may falsely believe it to be extremely large, but if I know that

17,163 is the largest number that is not the sum of the squares of distinct primes,

then I can characterize the content of his claim in *de re* form as:

The student claims **of** 17,163 that it is the sum of at most twenty-seven primes,

and can go on to draw inferences from that claim, to assess its plausibility in the light of the rest of my beliefs. (It is true, but only because *all* integers are the sum of at most twenty-seven primes.) Identifying what is being talked about permits me to extract information across a doxastic gap.

We saw originally in the treatment of truth assessments and knowledge the crucial difference between *attributing* a commitment and *undertaking* or acknowledging one. We now see what is involved in moving from the claim

It is true that Benjamin Franklin invented bifocals,

which is the undertaking of a commitment to the effect that Benjamin Franklin invented bifocals, via the undertaking of a commitment to the claim that Benjamin Franklin is the inventor of the lightning rod, to the claim

It is true **of** the inventor of the lightning rod that he invented bifocals.

(It is through this 'true of' locution that the earlier remarks about the essentially social structure of truth assessments connects with the account just offered of the social structure that underlies propositional attitude ascriptions *de re*.) Extracting information from the remarks of others requires grasping what is expressed when one offers *de re* characterizations of the contents of their beliefs—that is, to be able to tell what their beliefs would be true *of* if they were true. It is to grasp the *representational* content of their claims. The point I have been making is that doing this is just mastering the *social* dimension of their inferential articulation.

If we look at *de re* specifications of the content of *intentions*, we will see that the prediction or explanation of *success* of actions plays a role here similar to that of the assessment of *truth* in the case of *beliefs*. So we can have the *de dicto* ascription of an intention:

Nicole intends that she shoot a deer.

together with the *de re* ascription of a belief:

Nicole believes of that cow that it is a deer.

yielding the *de re* ascription of an intention:

Nicole intends of that cow that she shoot it.

We would appeal to these perspectivally different sorts of specifications of the content of her intention in order to explain different aspects of her behavior. If what we want to do is to predict or explain what Nicole is *trying* to do, we should use the *de dicto* specification of her intention and her belief. That will explain why she will pull the trigger. But if what we want to predict or explain is what she will *succeed* in doing, what will actually happen, then we should use the *de re* specifications. They will explain why she will shoot a cow, even though she wants only to shoot deer. Success of actions plays the same role as truth of claims, as far as concerns the difference between *de re* and *de dicto* specifications of the contents of intentional attitudes.

III. Conclusion

I have claimed that the primary representational locution in ordinary language, the one we use to talk about the representational dimension of our thought and talk, to specify what we are thinking and talking *about*, is *de re* ascriptions of propositional attitude. It is the role they play in such ascriptions that gives their meanings to the 'of' or 'about' we use to express intentional directedness. I have also claimed that the expressive role of these locutions is to make explicit the distinction of social perspective involved in keeping our books straight on who is committed to what. The social dimension of inference involved in the communication to others of claims that must be available as reasons both to the speaker and to the audience, in spite of differences in collateral commitments, is what underlies the representational dimension of discourse.

Beliefs and claims that are *propositionally* contentful are necessarily *representationally* contentful because their inferential articulation essentially involves a *social* dimension. That social dimension is unavoidable because the inferential significance of a claim, the appropriate antecedents and consequences of a doxastic commitment, depends on the background of collateral commitments available for service as auxiliary hypotheses. Thus any specification of a propositional content must be made from the perspective of some such set of commitments. One wants to say that the *correct* inferential role is determined by the collateral claims that are *true*. Just so; that is what *each* interlocutor wants to say: each has an at least slightly different perspective from which to evaluate inferential proprieties. Representational locutions make explicit the sorting of commitments into those attributed and those undertaken—without which communication would be impossible, given those differences of perspective. The *representational* dimension of propositional contents reflects the *social* structure of their *inferential* articulation in the game of giving and asking for reasons.

SIX

◆ ◆ ◆

Objectivity and the Normative Fine Structure of Rationality

I. Semantic Assertibilism

A basic pragmatist methodological thesis is that the point of the theoretical association of *meanings* with linguistic expressions is to explain the *use* of those expressions. (Semantics must answer to pragmatics.) A fundamental divide among theorists who agree in endorsing this methodological pragmatism then concerns the terms in which the use of linguistic expressions is understood. One camp takes as its explanatory target *proprieties* of use. Meanings are invoked to explain how it is *correct* or *appropriate* to use words and sentences, how one *ought* to deploy them. The other camp (Quinean behaviorists may serve as an example) insists on specifying the use to be explained in sparer terms. The ultimate explanatory target at which semantic theory aims is utterances and dispositions to utter described in a vocabulary resolutely restricted to nonnormative terms.[1] I will say something further along about why I think the second camp is misguided. But for now I just want to put this option to one side, with the observation that doing so does not by itself require relinquishing commitments to naturalistic semantics. For one might well accept a normative characterization of the explanatory target—specifying use in terms that permit one to distinguish, say, correct from incorrect representations of states of affairs—while retaining a commitment eventually to offering a reductive account of the origin and nature of those proprieties in turn, framed in the sort of modally rich but not explicitly normative vocabularies routinely employed in the special sciences, whether physical, biological, or social.[2]

The idea behind assertibility theories of the propositional contents expressed by declarative sentences is to start with a notion of linguistic propriety that could be understood in terms of allowable moves in a game. To specify the circumstances in which a sentence is assertible is to say when its assertional use is appropriate or allowable, when a speaker is licensed or entitled to use the sentence to perform that speech act, when its assertional utterance would have a certain sort of normative significance or status. Basing one's semantics on the association of sentences with assertibility conditions is not only a way of construing meaning as potentially explanatory of use. It is also an identification of meaning with a core feature of use—one, presumably, in terms of which other important dimensions of use can then be explained. The very tight connection that is envisaged between meaning, so construed, and proprieties of use is, I think, one of the sources of the attractiveness of broadly assertibilist approaches to meaning.

Another is the prospect of starting with relatively clear explanatory raw materials. The first obligation of the assertibility theorist will of course be to explain the notion of assertibility. Doing that requires first saying something about assertional force: about what it is for a speech act to have the significance of an assertion. The next requirement is to specify a sense of propriety appropriate to that speech act: to say what it is for an assertion to be appropriate or correct, for the speaker to be entitled or permitted to produce it. Neither of these tasks is simple or straightforward. But we do have a relatively familiar and unmysterious framework in which to address them. For the first takes its place as an instance of distinguishing different kinds of moves in a game; we are invited to think of asserting as a species in the same genus with punting, bidding, castling, betting, and so on. And the second takes its place as an instance of saying when moves of the specified kind are permitted. We should count ourselves fortunate indeed if we could, as the assertibilist hopes and promises, construct a workable concept of the meaning or content associated with declarative sentences (and hence also with the beliefs and judgments they express) from such raw materials.

The biggest challenge to this happy prospect stems from the fact that assertions are subject to two essential but fundamentally different kinds of normative appraisal. We can ask whether an assertion is correct in the sense that the speaker was entitled to make it, perhaps in virtue of having reasons, evidence, or some other sort of justification for it. This might be thought of as a way of asking whether the speaker is blameworthy for performing this speech act, whether the speaker has fulfilled the obligations the rules of the game specify as preconditions for making a move of this sort in the game. This is the normative aspect of use the assertibilist begins with. But we can also ask whether the assertion is correct in the sense of being *true*, in the sense that things are as it claims they are. It is a basic criterion of adequacy of a semantic theory that it explain this dimension of normative assessment, this normatively described aspect of use. The challenge to the sort of approach to semantics I have been calling 'assertibilist' is to show how the conceptual raw materials this approach allows itself can be deployed so as to underwrite attributions of propositional content for which this sort of *objective* normative assessment is intelligible.

The attempt by assertibility theorists to satisfy this central criterion of adequacy of semantic theories has typically taken the form of appeals to some sort of *ideality* condition. Assessments of truth are understood as assessments of assertibility under ideal conditions (what Sellars called 'semantic assertibility')—of what claims one would be entitled to or justified in making if one were an ideal knower, or given full information, maximal evidence, at the end of inquiry, and so on. I'm not going to argue the point here, but my own view is that this sort of strategy is hopeless.[3] If it is the best available, we should just give up the assertibilist project. In that case the obvious alternative is to start with a notion of meaning that directly underwrites normative assessments of objective representational correctness: truth conditions. We will not then be able to explain the association with linguistic expressions of semantic contents, so understood, by straightforward assimilation to making moves allowed by the rules defining a game, as promised by the alternative broadly assertibilist explanatory strategy. Attempts by truth-conditional semantic theorists to construct the other dimension of normative assessment of assertions—assertibility in the sense of entitlement, justification, having reasons or evidence—have typically taken the form of reliability theories. Assessments of assertibility in the sense of cognitive entitlement or justification are understood as assessments of objective or subjective likelihood of truth. In Chapter 3 I rehearsed some of the structural problems afflicting this sort of strategy as well.

What I want to do instead is to explore a different way in which one might start from the sort of normative statuses the assertibilist invokes, intelligible in terms of moves in a rule-governed game, and on that basis associate with declarative sentences propositional contents that are objective in the sense of swinging free of the attitudes of the linguistic practitioners who deploy them in assertions. The idea is roughly to split up the notion of assertibility into two parts. More precisely, where assertibility theorists appeal to just *one* sort of normative status—a sentence being assertible, or a speaker being justified or having sufficient reasons to assert it—I look at *two* kinds of normative status: commitment and entitlement. Discerning this additional normative structure in linguistic practice, in particular, exploiting the relations and interactions between these two kinds of normative status articulating the *force* or significance of linguistic performances, makes possible the specification of propositional *contents* with desirable properties.

Chief among these is the *objectivity*, in the sense of a specifiable sort of attitude-transcendence, of the propositional contents that are suitably defined in terms of the roles played by their bearers in linguistic practices characterized in terms of alterations and inheritance of commitments and entitlements. This result holds good even if the normative statuses of commitment and entitlement are themselves understood as *social* statuses, that is, as creatures of individual and communal attitudes.

II. Giving and Asking for Reasons

Semantic assertibilism is implicitly committed to demarcating specifically *linguistic* practices by restricting that term to practices that confer on some performances the significance of *claims* or *assertions*. What is assert*ed* in an act of assert*ing*, what is assert*ible*, is a propositional content. Assertible contents, assertibles, are also believables and judgeables; states of belief and acts of judgment can accordingly be expressed by assertions. Linguistic expressions whose freestanding utterances have the default significance of assertions are (declarative) sentences. My aim is to investigate the propositional contents that are associated with linguistic expressions by their playing this central role in assertional practices.

The first key idea is that a performance deserves to count as having the significance of an assertion only in the context of a set of social practices with the structure of (in Sellars's phrase) a *game of giving and asking for reasons*. Assertions are essentially performances that can both serve as and stand in need of reasons. Propositional contents are essentially what can serve as both premises and conclusions of inferences. This inferentialist idea might be called 'linguistic rationalism'.[4] Linguistic rationalism is not a standard part of the armamentarium of semantic assertibilism, but I think it is what is required to make that explanatory strategy work. I suggested in Chapter 1 what seem to me good reasons to see giving and asking for reasons as the defining core of discursive (concept-mongering) practice; I do not propose to rehearse them here. Rather, I want to treat linguistic rationalism as a hypothesis, and to explore its consequences.

In the rest of this chapter I make two arguments. First, in this section I argue that no set of practices is recognizable as a game of giving and asking for reasons for assertions unless it involves acknowledging at least two sorts of normative status, *commitments* and *entitlements,* and some general structures relating them. I show how we can understand practices incorporating those statuses in that structure as conferring propositional contents on linguistic expressions suitably caught up in them. Then, in the next section, I argue that propositional contents specified in terms of their contribution to the commitments and entitlements that articulate the normative significance of speech acts exhibiting those contents display *objectivity* of a particular sort: they are not about any constellation of attitudes on the part of the linguistic practitioners who produce and consume them as reasons.

Suppose we have a set of counters or markers such that producing or playing one has the social significance of making an assertional move in the game. We can call such counters 'sentences'. Then for any player at any time there must be a way of partitioning sentences into two classes, by distinguishing somehow those that he is disposed or otherwise prepared to assert (perhaps when suitably prompted). These counters, which are distinguished by bearing the player's mark, being on his list, or being kept in his box, constitute his score. By playing a new counter, making an assertion, one alters one's own score, and perhaps that of others.

Here is my first claim: for such a game or set of toy practices to be recognizable as involving assertions, it must be the case that playing one counter, or otherwise adding it to one's score, can *commit* one to playing others, or adding them to one's score. If one asserts, "The swatch is red," one *ought* to add to one's score also "The swatch is colored." Making the one move *obliges* one to be prepared to make the other as well. This is not to say that all players actually *do* have the dispositions they *ought* to have. One may not act as one is committed or obliged to act; one can break or fail to follow this sort of rule of the game, at least in particular cases, without thereby being expelled from the company of players of the asserting game. Still, I claim, assertional games must have rules of this sort: rules of *consequential commitment.*

Why? Because to be recognizable as assertional, a move must not be idle, it must make a difference, it must have consequences for what else it is appropriate to do, according to the rules of the game. Assertions express judgments or beliefs. Putting a sentence on one's list of judgments, putting it in one's belief box, has consequences for how one ought, rationally, to act, judge, and believe. We may be able to construct cases where it is intelligible to attribute beliefs that are consequentially inert and isolated from their fellows: "I just believe that cows look goofy, that's all. Nothing follows from that, and I am not obliged to act in any particular way on that belief." But *all* of our beliefs could not intelligibly be understood to be like this. If putting sentences onto my list or into my box *never* has consequences for what else belongs there, then we ought not to understand the list as consisting of all my judgments, or the box as containing all my beliefs. For in that case knowing what moves someone was disposed to make would tell us nothing else about that person.

Understanding a claim, the significance of an assertional move, requires understanding at least some of its consequences, knowing what else (what other moves) one would be committing oneself to by making that claim. A parrot, we can imagine, can produce an utterance perceptually indistinguishable from an assertion of "The swatch is red." Our nonetheless not taking it to have asserted that sentence, not to have made a move in that game, *is* our taking it that, unaware as it is of the inferential involvements of the claim that it would be expressing, of what it would be committing itself to were it to make the claim, it has not thereby succeeded in committing itself to anything. Making that assertion is committing oneself to such consequences as that the swatch is colored, that it is not green, and so on.

For this reason we can understand making a claim as taking up a particular sort of normative stance toward an inferentially articulated content. It is *endorsing* it, taking *responsibility* for it, *committing* oneself to it. The difference between treating something as a claiming and treating it just as a brute sounding-off, between treating it as making a move in the assertional game and treating it as an idle performance, is just whether one treats it as the undertaking of a commitment that is suitably articulated by its consequential relations to other commitments. These are *rational* relations, whereby undertaking one commitment *rationally* obliges one to undertake others, related to it as its inferential consequences. These relations articulate the *content* of the commitment or responsibility one undertakes by asserting a sentence. Apart from such relations, there is no such content, hence no assertion.

I have been belaboring what is perhaps an obvious point. Not just any way of distinguishing some sentences from others can be understood as distinguishing those asserted, those that express judgments or beliefs from the rest. For putting a sentence on a list or in a box to be intelligible as asserting or believing it, doing so must at least have the significance of committing or obliging one to make other moves of a similar sort, with sentences that (thereby) count as inferentially related to the original. Absent such consequential commitments, the game lacks the rational structure required for us to understand its moves as the making of contentful assertions.

The next claim I want to make is that practices incorporating a game of giving and asking for reasons—*rational* practices, which linguistic rationalism supposes to be the only ones that deserve to be thought of as *linguistic* practices—must involve acknowledgment of a *second* kind of normative status. We have said that making a move in the assertional game should be understood as acknowledging a certain sort of *commitment*, articulated by consequential inferential relations linking the asserted sentence to other sentences. But players of the game of giving and asking for reasons must also distinguish among the commitments an interlocutor undertakes, a distinguished subclass to which she is *entitled*. Linguistic rationalism understands assertions, the fundamental sort of speech act, as essentially things that can both serve as and stand in need of reasons. Giving reasons for a claim is producing other assertions that *license* or *entitle* one to it, that *justify* it. Asking for reasons for a claim is asking for its warrant, for what entitles one to that commitment. Such a practice presupposes a distinction between assertional commitments to which one is entitled and those to which one is not entitled. Reason-giving practices make sense only if there can be an issue as to whether or not practitioners are entitled to their commitments.

Indeed, I take it that liability to demands for justification—that is, demonstration of entitlement—is another major dimension of the responsibility one undertakes, the commitment one makes, in asserting something. In making an assertion one implicitly acknowledges the propriety, at least under some circumstances, of demands for reasons, for justification of the claim one has endorsed, the commitment one has undertaken. Besides the *committive* dimension of assertional practice, there is the *critical* dimension: the aspect of the practice in which the propriety of those commitments is assessed. Apart from this critical dimension, the notion of *reasons* gets no grip.

So the overall claim is that the sense of endorsement that determines the force of assertional speech acts involves, at a minimum, a kind of *commitment* the speaker's *entitlement* to which is always potentially at issue. The assertible contents expressed by declarative sentences whose utterance can have this sort of force must accordingly be inferentially articulated along both normative dimensions. Downstream, they must have inferential *consequences*, commitment to which is entailed by commitment to the original content. Upstream, they must have inferential *antecedents,* relations to contents that can serve as premises from which entitlement to the original content can be inherited.

These two flavors of normative status are not simply independent of each other. They interact. For the entitlements at issue are entitlements to commitments. We can say that two assertible contents are *incompatible* in case *commitment* to one precludes *entitlement* to the other. Thus commitment to the content expressed by the sentence "The swatch is red" rules out entitlement to the commitment that would be undertaken by asserting the sentence "The swatch is green." Incompatibilities among the *contents* expressed by sentences, derived from the interaction of the two normative dimensions articulating the *force* of assertions of those sentences, induce their own sort of inferential relation. For we can associate with each sentence the set of all the sentences that are incompatible with it, according to the rules of the particular assertional game of giving and asking for reasons within which it plays a role. Inclusion relations among these sets then correspond to inferential relations among the sentences. That is, the content of the claim expressed by asserting "The swatch is vermilion" entails the content of the claim expressed by asserting "The swatch is red," because everything incompatible with being red is incompatible with being vermilion.[5]

So the two sorts of normative status that must be in play in practices that incorporate a game of giving and asking for reasons, commitment and entitlement, induce *three* sorts of inferential relations in the assertible contents expressed by sentences suitably caught up in those practices:

> *committive* (that is, commitment-preserving) inferences, a category that generalizes deductive inference;
> *permissive* (that is, entitlement-preserving) inferences, a category that generalizes inductive inference; and
> *incompatibility* entailments, a category that generalizes modal (counterfactual-supporting) inference.

It can be argued on relatively general grounds, though I will not do so here, that these three sorts of inferential consequence relation can be ranked strictly by their strength: all incompatibility entailments are commitment-preserving (though not vice versa), and all commitment-preserving inferences are entitlement-preserving (though not vice versa).

This is what in the title of the chapter I call "the normative fine structure of rationality." Rational practices, practices that include the production and consumption of reasons—the "giving and asking for reasons" of the Sellarsian slogan with which we began—must distinguish two sorts of normative status: a kind of *commitment*, undertaken by the assertional speech acts by which alone anything can be put forward *as* a reason, and a kind of *entitlement*, which is what is at issue when a reason is requested or required. This normative fine structure is *inferentially articulated* along three axes, defined by inheritance of commitment, inheritance of entitlement, and entailments according to the incompatibilities defined by the interactions of commitments and entitlements.

The core idea behind assertibility theories was a pragmatist one. It is to start with something we *do*—specifically, to start with the fundamental speech act of *assertion*, with the notion of assertional *force*—and to read off a notion of *content* (what we say or think) directly from proprieties governing that sort of speech act. Thus the content expressed by declarative sentences was to be identified and articulated in terms of assertibility conditions, that is, conditions under which it would be *appropriate* to assert the sentence. I have suggested that in the context of a commitment to linguistic rationalism, to the idea that the game of giving and asking for reasons is the home language game of assertion, this undifferentiated normative notion of the propriety of an assertion can be replaced by a more finely articulated normative structure. For the game of giving and asking for reasons reveals itself as involving two different sorts of normative status (and so normative assessment). The score we must keep on those who engage in practices that include giving and asking for reasons has two components: we must keep track of what they are *committed* to, and also of which of these commitments they are *entitled* to.

Making this refinement at the level of the *pragmatic* theory, the theory of assertional *force,* induces corresponding refinements at the level of *semantic* theory, the theory of assertible *content.* For now instead of the undifferentiated question "Under what circumstances would it be appropriate to assert the sentence?" we must ask, "Under what circumstances (for instance, in the context of what other claims) would one count as *committed* to the claim expressed by the sentence?" and "Under what circumstances (for instance, in the context of what other claims) would one count as *entitled* to the claim?" Indeed, it appears that we should look not only upstream, by asking what claims or circumstances commit or entitle us to the claim in question, but also downstream, by asking to what else the claim in question commits or entitles us as *consequences.* Further, we should take account of the interaction of these two normative dimensions into which we have subdivided the undifferentiated notion of assertibility or appropriate assertion by asking also with what other claims the claim in question is *incompatible.* This structure gives broadly assertibilist semantic theories—those that seek to derive a notion of semantic content directly from the proprieties of use that are the subject matter in the first instance of pragmatics—a great deal more to work with.

III. Objectivity

What I want to do in this final section is to demonstrate one of the semantic payoffs that this richer pragmatic structure enables.

Assertibilist semantic theories seek to understand propositional content by associating with sentences as their semantic interpretants *assertibility conditions:* circumstances under which the sentence in question is appropriately assertible. The attraction of such theories is due to the very close tie they establish between meaning and use. They hold out the promise of reading *semantic* norms directly off of *pragmatic* ones, that is, off of the rules for the asserting game, or the norms implicitly acknowledged by those who participate in assertional practice. The challenge for them is to get out the other end of their machinery a sense of 'correct' that is sufficiently objective to be recognizable as a notion of propositional content. On the face of it, assertional speech acts are subject to two central sorts of normative appraisal. One asks whether the speech act was appropriate in light of the attitudes of the practitioners: Was all available evidence taken into account? Were the inferences made good ones, as far as the practitioners know? In general, did the speaker follow the rules of the game, so as not to be blameworthy for producing the assertion? The other sort of appraisal swings free of the attitudes of the practitioners and looks instead to the subject matter about which claims are made for the applicable norms. Here the central question is: Is the claim correct in the sense that things really are as it says they are? Only an omniscient being could follow a rule enjoining practitioners to make only claims that are true. This means that the conduct of those who, through no fault of their own, make false claims is not blameworthy. Nonetheless, this further sort of appraisal is possible.

So theories of this sort face a structural dilemma. In order to make their raw materials as intelligible as possible, one wants to tie assertibility closely to people's attitudes, to what they *take* to be assertible or *treat as* assertible. This need not take the extreme form of identifying the assertibility conditions of sentences with nonnormatively specified conditions under which practitioners are disposed to assert those sentences. But there is pressure to make whatever norms are invoked be ones that can be read off of the attitudes of practitioners who apply and acknowledge the applicability of those norms. Yet the more closely the norms of assertibility that articulate the contents associated with sentences reflect the attitudes of those who use the sentences, the farther they will be from the sort of objective norms appealed to in assessments of representational correctness, of getting things right according to a standard set by the things about which one is speaking. If 'assertible' is read as requiring correctness in this more objective sense, then assertibility conditions just become truth conditions, and the link to the attitudes and practices of those who use the sentences to make claims, which promised to make the association of sentences with semantic content intelligible, becomes correspondingly obscured. So the challenge for assertibility theories is to start with a notion of propriety of assertion that is grounded in and intelligible in terms of the practice of speakers and audiences, and yet which is rich enough to fund normative assessments that are objective in the sense of transcending the attitudes of practitioners.

Consider an example of the sort that standardly causes trouble for assertibility theories. Whenever

  1. "The swatch is red"

is appropriately assertible, it is equally appropriate to assert

  2. "The claim that the swatch is red is properly assertible by me now."

For the latter just makes explicit, as part of the content that is assert*ed,* what it is implicit in what one is doing in the former assert*ing.* And yet we want to say that the contents are different. Though the two claims have the same *assertibility* conditions, they have different *truth* conditions. For the swatch could *be* red without my being in a position to *say* that it is. And surely we could describe circumstances in which I would have extremely good evidence that the swatch was red, so that (1) is assertible for me, even though it in fact was not red—perhaps even in circumstances where the swatch does not exist. It seems that assertibility theories are leaving out something important.

But things look different if we help ourselves to the finer-grained normative vocabulary of commitment and entitlement, and hence of incompatibility. We see that (1) and (2) would be incompatibility-equivalent (in the sense that they incompatibility-entail each other) just in case everything incompatible with (1) were incompatible with (2), and vice versa. But in the situations just described, this is precisely not so. To say that the swatch could be red without my being in a position to say that it is, is to say that some claims are incompatible with (1) being assertible by me now that are not incompatible with (1). For instance,

3. "I do not exist," or
4. "Rational beings never evolved"

are both incompatible with (2) but not with (1). And to say that there are circumstances in which I would have extremely good evidence that (1) is true, so that it is appropriately assertible by me, even though (1) is not in fact true, is just to say there are claims that are incompatible with (1), but not with its being assertible by me. But

5. "In the absence of a swatch, but otherwise in circumstances that are perceptually quite standard, my optic nerve is being stimulated just as it would be if there were a red swatch in front of me"

might qualify. The additional normative expressive resources made available by distinguishing the status of being assertionally *committed* from that of being *entitled* to such a commitment are sufficient to distinguish the contents of ordinary claims from those of claims about what is assertible.

One might worry that this result is not robust, but depends on setting up the test case in terms of the undifferentiated notion of appropriate assertibility, while assessing it using the more specific normative notions of commitment and entitlement (and so incompatibility). This thought suggests that better test cases would be provided by

2′. "I am now committed to the claim that the swatch is red," and
2″. "I am now entitled to the claim that the swatch is red."

But in fact this additional specificity makes no difference. (3) and (4) are incompatible with both (2′) and (2″), just as they were with (2), though not incompatible with (1). And (5), or some variant of it, is still incompatible with (1), but not with (2′) or (2″).

In fact, looking at (2′) and (2″) offers some insight into *why* distinguishing the normative statuses of commitment and entitlement offers an important expressive advance in broadly assertibilist semantic theories, when compared with the vaguer notion of assertibility. For although one is *committed* to (2′) whenever one is *committed* to (1), one is not *entitled* to those claims in all the same circumstances. In particular, I can be *entitled* to (2′) just on the basis of a rehearsal of my commitments, perhaps by noticing that I just asserted (1), without needing to investigate the colors of swatches. But I can become *entitled* to (1) only by an investigation of just that sort. In the other case it is not at all clear even that one is *entitled* to (2″) whenever one is entitled to (1). Insofar as reliabilism is correct (what I called the Founding Insight of reliabilism in Chapter 3), I can *be* entitled to claims without having good reason to *believe* that I am so entitled. But even if that is wrong, and entitlements to claims of the form of (2″) do go along with entitlements to base-level claims such as (1), the two sorts of claims are still distinguishable in terms of the *commitments* they involve. For surely one could be *committed* to the claim that the swatch is red, that is, to (1), without thereby being committed to the claim that one is *entitled* to it. In general, one *ought* to be entitled to one's commitments, but the game of giving and asking for reasons has a point precisely insofar as we must distinguish between commitments to which one is entitled and those to which one is not. So one must at least allow that it is *possible* that one is in such a situation in any particular case. Again, (2″) and (1) do not evidently have the same commitment-inferential *consequences*. The condtional

6. "If the swatch is red, then the swatch is red"

is evidently correct in that it codifies a commitment-preserving inference. (The stuttering inference is as safe as any could be.) By contrast, the conditional

7. "If I am entitled to the claim that the swatch is red, then the swatch is red"

is not one that ought to be endorsed as correct in the sense of commitment-preserving, at least for any notion of entitlement that humans can secure regarding empirical matters of fact. It is, after all, an instance of the very implausible schema

8. "If *S* is entitled to the claim that the swatch is red, then the swatch is red."

Now, I have been careful to be as noncommittal as possible regarding the specifics of the notions of commitment and entitlement (and hence incompatibility) employed in discussing these examples. For that reason, some of my particular claims about what are and are not good inferences, in any of the three fundamental senses of the permissive, committive, or incompatibility entailments, will be controversial for those who have in mind some particular ways of thinking about commitment and (especially) entitlement. But worries about these details will not affect the overall point I am after. For that is that notions of commitment and entitlement (and hence of incompatibility) *can* be put in play so as rigorously and systematically to distinguish between the contents of ordinary empirical claims and the contents of any claims about who is committed or entitled to what. The fact that other ways of deploying the notions of commitment and entitlement would *not* allow all of those distinctions is neither here nor there; it would just provide a good reason not to use *those* notions of commitment and entitlement.

The fact is that the distinction between sentences sharing *assertibility* conditions and sharing *truth* conditions, illustrated, for instance, by sentences such as

9. "I will write a book about Hegel," and
10. "I foresee that I will write a book about Hegel,"

which are alike in the first way but not in the second, can be made out in terms of commitments and entitlements, without the need to invoke the notion of truth. I may be *committed* to (9) and (10) in the same circumstances, and may even be *entitled* to them in the same circumstances; we could regiment the use of 'foresee' so as to ensure this. But

11. "I will die in the next ten minutes"

will still be incompatible with (9) and not with (10), for any notion of foreseeing that does not entail omniscience.[6] And we should not be surprised by this result. For the *consequences* of (9) and (10) are quite different.

12. "If I will write a book about Hegel, then I will write a book about Hegel"

is, once again, as secure an inference as one could wish.

13. "If I foresee that I will write a book about Hegel, then I will write a book about Hegel,"

by contrast, is a conditional whose plausibility depends on how good I am at foreseeing. (There are lots of orphaned "Volume I"s about, after all.) Even though the commitment made explicit in the antecedent of (13) *is* the commitment expressed in the consequent, there are claims, such as (11), that are incompatible with its consequent and not incompatible with its antecedent. The difference in content between (9) and (10), which we are accustomed to think of as a difference in truth conditions (compatible with the identity of their assertibility conditions), just is the difference in their consequences, encapsulated in the different status of the conditionals (12) and (13). And that difference manifests itself in a difference in the claims that are incompatible with (9) and (10), a notion we can understand entirely in terms of the normative statuses of commitment and entitlement. Put another way, looking at propositional content in terms of incompatibilities, themselves defined in terms of the fundamental normative statuses of commitment and entitlement, provides the expressive resources to distinguish between the sense of 'assertible' that falls short of guaranteeing truth (as 'foresee' does), and the sense (perennially sought in terms of some sort of 'ideal' entitlement, in a sense of 'ideal' that removes it substantially from actual practices of giving and asking for reasons) that would guarantee truth. This is the sense of "It is assertible that . . ." that would be redundant, in that the incompatibilities associated with "It is assertible that p" would be just those associated with p as they are for "It is *true* that p."

The point of all this is that the *objectivity* of propositional content—the fact that in claiming that the swatch is red we are not saying anything about who could appropriately assert anything, or about who is committed or entitled to what, are indeed saying something that could be true even if there had never been rational beings—is a feature we can make intelligible as a structure of the commitments and entitlements that articulate the use of sentences: of the norms, in a broad sense, that govern the practice of asserting, the game of giving and asking for reasons. And we can make sense of practices having that structure even if we understand commitment and entitlement as themselves *social* statuses, instituted by the attitudes of linguistic practitioners. *All* that is required is that the commitments and entitlements they associate with ordinary empirical claims such as "The swatch is red" generate incompatibilities for these claims that differ suitably from those associated with any claims about who is committed to, entitled to, or in a position to assert anything. The recognition of propositional contents that are objective in this sense is open to any community whose inferentially articulated practices acknowledge the different normative statuses of commitment and entitlement. I argued in the previous section that this includes all *rational* communities—all of those whose practices include the game of giving and asking for reasons. According to the thesis of linguistic rationalism, this is all linguistic communities whatsoever. I have tried here to explain how we can begin to understand the objectivity of our thought—the way in which the contents of our thought go beyond the attitudes of endorsement or entitlement we have toward those contents—as a particular aspect of the normative fine structure of rationality.[7]

Notes

◆ ◆ ◆

Introduction

1. Michael Dummett, *Frege's Philosophy of Language* (New York: Harper and Row, 1973), p. 362.

2. Donald Davidson, "Thought and Talk," in *Inquiries into Truth and Interpretation* (New York: Oxford University Press, 1984), p. 156.

3. This is not exactly the same as what in Chapter 1 I call 'representationalism', which concerns commitment to a more specific reductive order of semantic explanation.

4. A theme adumbrated in M. H. Abrams's classic work *The Mirror and the Lamp: Romantic Theory and the Critical Tradition* (New York: Oxford University Press, 1953).

5. Cf. Isaiah Berlin's discussion in *Vico and Herder: Two Studies in the History of Ideas* (New York: Viking Press, 1976).

6. Of course, as is generally true with the methodological oppositions considered here, one need not take either element as autonomously intelligible and try to account for the other in terms of it. One may instead simply explore and unpack the relations among the different aspects.

7. Here I speak with the vulgar, so as to avoid lengthy paraphrase. 'Experience' is not one of my words. I did not find it necessary to use it in the many pages of *Making It Explicit* (though it is mentioned), and the same policy prevails in the body of this work. I do not see

that we need—either in epistemology or, more important, in semantics—to appeal to any intermediaries between perceptible facts and
reports of them that are noninferentially elicited by the exercise of
reliable differential responsive dispositions. There are, of course,
many *causal* intermediaries, since the noninferential observation
report is a propositionally contentful commitment the acknowledgment of which stands at the end of a whole causal chain of reliably
covarying events, including a cascade of neurophysiological ones.
But I do not see that any of these has any particular conceptual or
(therefore) cognitive or semantic significance. The strongest arguments to the contrary, from the point of view presented in this work,
are those presented by my colleague John McDowell in *Mind and
World* (Cambridge, Mass.: Harvard University Press, 1994).

 8. Wilfrid Sellars, *Action, Knowledge, and Reality,* ed. H. N. Castaneda
    (Indianapolis: Bobbs-Merrill, 1975), p. 285.

 9. I tell such a story in more detail in the first three chapters of *Making
    It Explicit* (Cambridge, Mass.: Harvard University Press, 1994).

10. Sellars's seminal inferentialist tract "Inference and Meaning," in
    *Pure Pragmatism and Possible Worlds: The Early Essays of Wilfrid
    Sellars,* ed. J. Sich (Reseda Calif.: Ridgeview Publishing, 1980),
    pp. 257–286, does not make these distinctions. Accordingly it may be
    subject to the criticism that it assembles evidence for weak inferen-
    tialism, and then treats it as justifying a commitment to strong infer-
    entialism, or even hyperinferentialism.

11. In his Introduction to the recent reprinting of Sellars's *Empiricism
    and the Philosophy of Mind,* to which I contributed a Study Guide
    (Cambridge, Mass.: Harvard University Press, 1997).

12. John Haugeland, "Heidegger on Being a Person," *Nous* 16 (1982):
    16–26.

13. Peirce is, on this issue as on so many others, a more complicated case.

14. As a quick gesture at the sort of thing I have in mind, consider
    adverbs. A verb such as 'walks' can be assigned a function from
    objects to sets of possible worlds as its semantic interpretant. Then an
    adverb such as 'slowly' can be assigned a function from [functions
    from objects to sets of possible worlds] to [functions from objects to

sets of possible worlds]. It is then a straightforward matter to represent the semantic difference between attributive and nonattributive adverbs: the difference between adverbs such as 'slowly', where the inference from 'a Fs' to 'a Fs slowly' is a good one, and adverbs such as 'in one's imagination', where the corresponding inference is not a good one. See, for example, David Lewis's "General Semantics," in *Semantics of Natural Language,* ed. G. Harman and D. Davidson (Dordrecht: Reidel, 1972), pp. 169–218.

15. Cf. chap. 3 of Charles Taylor's *Hegel* (New York: Cambridge University Press, 1975).

16. Hegel is not always read as addressing the topics I see as central to his work—primarily regarding the nature of conceptual norms and conceptual content. But when he is so read, he turns out to have a great deal of interest to say. Developing and justifying this interpretive line is a major undertaking. I foresee that I will write a book about Hegel.

17. Versions of some of these lectures have been published in other places. An early rendering of Chapter 1 appeared as "Inference, Expression, and Induction: Sellarsian Themes," *Philosophical Studies* 54 (1988): 257–285. A fuller account appears as Chapter 2 of *Making It Explicit.* Chapter 2 of this book appeared in *Philosophical Perspectives* 12 (1998): 127–139, *Language, Mind, and Ontology,* ed. James Tomberlin. A fuller account is given in the second half of Chapter 4 of *Making It Explicit.* Chapter 3 was published in *Monist* 81, no. 3 (July 1998): 371–392, *Reunifying Epistemology.* The general line of thought develops themes from the first half of Chapter 4 of *Making It Explicit.* Chapter 4 presents the central argument of Chapter 6 of *Making It Explicit.* A version of Chapter 5 was published as "Reasoning and Representing," in Michaelis Michael and John O'Leary-Hawthorne, eds., *Philosophy in Mind: The Place of Philosophy in the Study of Mind* (Dordrecht: Kluwer Academic Publishers, 1994), pp. 159–178. It and Chapter 6 both develop themes from Chapter 8 of *Making It Explicit.*

18. An inferentialist approach to the expressive role characteristic of this sort of locution is offered in Chapter 5 of *Making It Explicit.*

1. Semantic Inferentialism and Logical Expressivism

1. Gottlob Frege, *Begriffsschrift* (1879) [hereafter *BGS*], section 3.

2. Michael Dummett, *Frege's Philosophy of Language* [hereafter *FPL*] (New York: Harper and Row, 1973), p. 432.

3. Ibid., p. 433. A few comments on this passage. First, the "deleterious effects in logic" Dummett has in mind include taking logics to be individuated by their theorems rather than their consequence relations. Although one can do things either way for classical logic, in more interesting cases logics can have the same theorems but different consequence relations. Second, the contrast with *analytic* is not obviously *contingent:* why rule out the possibility of necessity that is not conceptual, but, say, physical? Third, the closing claim seems historically wrong. Kant already distinguished analytic from synthetic judgments, and his concerns did not evidently stem from concern with the subject matter of logic. I include the passage anyway, since I think the shift in emphasis Dummett is endorsing is a good one, although the reasons he advances need filling in and cleaning up.

4. Wilfrid Sellars, "Inference and Meaning," reprinted in *Pure Pragmatics and Possible Worlds* [hereafter *PPPW*], ed. J. Sicha (Reseda, Calif.: Ridgeview Publishing Co., 1980), p. 261.

5. Ibid., p. 265.

6. Ibid., p. 284.

7. Wilfrid Sellars, "Language, Rules, and Behavior," in *PPPW,* footnote 2 to p. 136.

8. Gottlob Frege, "Boole's Logical Calculus and the Concept-Script," in *Posthumous Writings* [hereafter *PW*], ed. H. Hermes, F. Kambartel, and F. Kaulbach (Chicago: University of Chicago Press, 1979), pp. 12–13.

9. Ibid., p. 13.

10. Ibid., p. 46.

11. Gottlob Frege, Preface to *BGS,* in *From Frege to Gödel,* ed. Jean van Heijenoort (Cambridge, Mass.: Harvard University Press, 1967), p. 7.

12. Frege, *PW,* p. 16.

13. Dummett, *FPL,* p. 453.

14. Ibid., p. 455.

15. Ibid., pp. 453–454.

16. Ibid., pp. 456–457.
17. Ibid., p. 454.
18. A. N. Prior, "The Runabout Inference Ticket," *Analysis* 21 (December 1960): 38–39.
19. Nuel D. Belnap, "Tonk, Plonk, and Plink," *Analysis* 22 (June 1962): 130–134.
20. Ibid.
21. Ibid., p. 455n.
22. Ibid., p. 358.

2. Action, Norms, and Practical Reasoning

1. Robert B. Brandom, *Making It Explicit* (Cambridge, Mass.: Harvard University Press, 1994). The ideas presented here are discussed there in more detail in the second half of Chapter 4.
2. G. E. M. Anscombe, *Intention* (Oxford: Blackwell, 1959); and Donald Davidson, originally in "Actions, Reasons, and Causes," reprinted in *Actions and Events* (New York: Oxford University Press, 1984).
3. Not necessarily a *description*, at least if that category is conceived narrowly. For, as will emerge in Section V of this chapter, it is important that the specifications in question can include *demonstrative* and indexical elements.
4. This is how the author of *Making It Explicit* writes his carefully defined version of ˢscare quotesˢ. The explicit theory of what they express can be found at pp. 545–547 of that work. The general idea is that by using such quote marks, the one uttering the sentence is *undertaking* responsibility for the claim being made, but only *attributing* to someone else the responsibility for these words being a good way to specify its content. So understood, such a quotation device is the converse of *de re* ascriptions of propositional attitude, as they are explained in Chapter 5 of this book.
5. Wilfrid Sellars, "Inference and Meaning," reprinted in *Pure Pragmatics and Possible Worlds: The Early Essays of Wilfrid Sellars,* ed. J. Sicha (Reseda, Calif.: Ridgeview Publishing, 1980), pp. 257–286.
6. In particular, the notion of the sort of commitment undertaking by making a claim that is elaborated in Chapter 3 of *Making It Explicit*.

7. *Critique of Practical Judgment*, sec. 7.

8. Wilfrid Sellars, "Thought and Action," in *Freedom and Determinism*, ed. Keith Lehrer (New York: Random House, 1966), p. 110.

9. I discuss Sellars on 'seems' in my study guide, included in Wilfrid Sellars, *Empiricism and the Philosophy of Mind* (Cambridge, Mass.: Harvard University Press, 1997), in the commentary to Section 16, pp. 139–144. I discuss the parallel with 'try' in *Making It Explicit*, pp. 294–295.

10. Donald Davidson, "Intending," in *Actions and Events*, pp. 100–101.

3. Insights and Blindspots of Reliabilism

1. The expectation or prediction need not rise to the level of perfect *certainty*. Although there may well be a use of 'knows' that requires such certainty, it was one of the great advances in twentieth-century epistemology prior to the advent of reliabilism to realize that such a concept of knowledge not only includes an unrefusable invitation to skepticism, but also is of no use for discussing the achievements of science, and in any case is not obligatory. If our ordinary use of 'know' involves such commitments, that is the best possible reason to replace it by a less committive technical notion that is more useful for our central epistemological purposes. The fact that there are circumstances in which we would have been wrong should not preclude our counting as knowing in the cases where we are in fact right. Our fallibility should not be taken to rule out the possibility of knowledge.

2. According to this line of thought, one can know something without knowing that one knows. (The $Kp \to KKp$ principle fails.) One might believe that p without believing that one knows that p. For, as in the example of the potsherds, one may not even believe that the belief is the outcome of a reliable process, though it is. The attitude of the believer might be that the belief she finds herself with perceptually just happened in this case to be true. Since belief is a condition for knowledge, if one does not even *believe* that one knows that p, then one does not *know* that one knows it.

3. Classical justificatory internalism about knowledge should be taken to require only that the candidate knower could give reasons for her belief, not that the belief in fact has been acquired as the result of antecedent consideration of those reasons. For the stronger requirement would limit knowledge to beliefs acquired inferentially. But we ought to be able to allow that *non*inferentially acquired beliefs—for instance, those acquired perceptually (and, arguably, by memory or even testimony)—can constitute genuine knowledge. The requirement would just be that after the fact the believer can offer reasons for her belief, for instance, by invoking her own reliability as a noninferential reporter.

4. It is tempting to overgeneralize from this platitude (in much the same way as it is from the Founding Insight of reliabilism) by seeking to *define* first the *truth* (and then in turn the *truth conditions*) of beliefs in terms of conduciveness to success of actions based on those beliefs. There are insuperable objections to such an explanatory strategy, which I have discussed in "Unsuccessful Semantics," *Analysis* 54, no. 3 (July 1994): 175–178.

5. This is Sellars's strategy for defending justificatory internalism, in "Empiricism and the Philosophy of Mind." See the discussion of this point in my study guide to Wilfrid Sellars, *Empiricism and the Philosophy of Mind*, (Cambridge, Mass.: Harvard University Press, 1997).

6. "Having reasons" rather than "being able to give reasons," because justificatory internalism need not be committed to withholding attributions of knowledge in cases where the possessor of reasons (in the form of other justified beliefs from which the belief in question follows) is de facto unable to produce them, say, through having forgotten them.

7. For a more nuanced discussion, see my treatment of Sellars's account of the logic of 'looks', in the study guide to *Empiricism and the Philosophy of Mind*.

8. Semantic programs such as those of Dretske, Fodor, and Millikan are at their weakest when addressing the question of what distinguishes representations that deserve to be called 'beliefs' from other sorts of indicating states.

9. These are not equivalent characterizations: broadly naturalistic explanations need not restrict themselves to the language of physics. But for the purposes of the argument here, the differences do not make a difference.

10. Alvin Goldman, "Discrimination and Perceptual Knowledge," *Journal of Philosophy* 73, no. 20 (1976): 771–791.

11. I say 'classical' because it is open to an internalist to deny that in such cases (and in all corresponding cases of the generic 'Twin Earth' type) the *internal* states are the same in the veridical and the non-veridical cases. *All* the two cases have in common is that the subject cannot tell them apart. But this fact need not be construed as sufficient to identify their contents. This is the option that McDowell pursues.

12. For an argument that these two sorts of normative status are essential elements of any game of giving and asking for reasons, see Chapter 6.

13. Chapter 5 explores some of the consequences of this social perspectival articulation of normative attitudes.

14. Robert B. Brandom, *Making It Explicit* (Cambridge, Mass.: Harvard University Press, 1994), esp. chaps. 3, 4, and 5.

4. What Are Singular Terms, and Why Are There Any?

1. Strictly, what is referred to by a singular term is a particular. Not all particulars are *objects:* there are also events, processes, and so on. The present argument does not turn on the differences among these sorts of particulars, and it will often be more convenient simply to talk of objects, where in fact any sort of particular can be involved.

2. W. V. O. Quine, *Word and Object* (Cambridge, Mass.: MIT Press, 1960), p. 96, emphasis added; see also p. 90.

3. Gottlob Frege, *Grundlagen,* Intro. secs. 46, 60, 62; in English, *Foundations of Arithmetic,* trans. J. L. Austin (New York: Harper and Row, 1960).

4. Gottlob Frege, "Compound Thoughts," *Mind* 72 (1963): 1.

5. In a sense, of course, we do not know how many such sentences there are, even restricting ourselves to a basic vocabulary, since we do

not have a syntactically adequate grammar for any natural language. But there are grammars that will generate *only* sentences of English. The difficult thing is getting one that will generate *all* of them, without generating all sorts of garbage as well.

6. For instance, Donald Davidson emphasizes this point in his influential "Theories of Meaning and Learnable Languages," reprinted in Donald Davidson, *Inquiries into Truth and Interpretation* (Oxford: Clarendon Press, 1984), pp. 3–16.

7. Notice that the problem of projection such a strategy addresses concerns moving from *proprieties* governing the use of one set of sentences to proprieties governing the use of a superset. A quite different issue concerns the relation between the correct use even of the sentences in the initial subset, on the one hand, and the actual occasions of use or dispositions of the community to use them. These puzzles must be sharply separated, for the first remains within the normative dimension, asking after the relation between two different sets of practically embodied norms, while the second asks after the relation between such norms and the nonnormative happenings that express them.

8. Roughly the direction taken in my *Making It Explicit* (Cambridge, Mass.: Harvard University Press, 1994).

9. Type/token issues are suppressed for the purposes of this chapter.

10. This requirement is not absolute. My "Singular Terms and Sentential Sign Designs," *Philosophical Topics* 15, no. 1 (Spring 1987): 125–167 (referred to hereafter as "STSSD"), shows how to make do just with substitutional relations among substituted-in expressions and how to do without antecedently distinguishable substituted-for expressions.

11. Strictly speaking, this is true only of what Dummett calls 'complex' predicates, by contrast to 'simple' ones, about which more later in this chapter. But as Dummett points out in making the distinction, Frege "tacitly assimilated simple predicates to complex ones." Michael Dummett, *Frege's Philosophy of Language* (New York: Harper and Row, 1973), p. 30.

12. From Frege's mature point of view, this qualification does not need to be made: sentences *are* singular terms, and the frames *are* predicates.

This is what motivates Frege's classification of sentences as singular terms. As will be pointed out later in this chapter, this need not be the whole story about sentences, a fact that immunizes Frege somewhat from Dummett's scandalized response to this point. Qua subsentential expressions, sentences are singular terms; the thesis is innocent of the objectionable implications Dummett complains about (missing the special role of sentences as usable to make moves in the language game—as though Frege had no idea of force, and as though being a name of the True or the False did not play a very special role for him) because sentences are not *essentially* subsentential expressions, and it is not as subsentential expressions that they have their special pragmatic position. (I am grateful to John McDowell for pointing this out.)

13. This point is distinct from, although related to, the distinction Dummett makes, in chap. 2 of *Frege's Philosophy of Language,* between simple and complex predicates. Dummett there points out (following Geach's discussion in "Quine on Classes and Properties" (*Philosophical Review* 62 [1953]: 409–412) that there is no simple *part* or subexpression common to "Rousseau admired Rousseau" and "Kant admired Kant" that is not also a part of "Kant admired Rousseau." Yet the first two share with each other a complex predicate that they do not share with the third. One of Frege's great discoveries was that one must be able to discern predicates in this sense (complex, or substitutionally derived ones) in order to appreciate the inferential role of sentences like "Anyone who admires someone admires himself." For one must appreciate the different patterns they instantiate in order to see that in the context of that quantificational claim, "Kant admired Rousseau" entails "Kant admired Kant." Thus the status of predicates as playing derived substitution-structural roles is what lies behind the second of Strawson's stigmata distinguishing predicates from singular terms: that they are subject to quantification. Concern with quantification, in particular with codifying the inferential role of quantificational claims, enforces the distinction between simple and complex predicates, between expressions that can be substituted for and those that are substitutional frames. But the need for this dis-

tinction is not, as Dummett claims (*Frege's Philosophy of Language*, pp. 28, 30), simply a consequence of the presence of quantificational locutions in a language. Complex predicates must be discerned by anyone who has mastered the sort of pattern of inference that is typically made explicit by a quantificational expression such as $(x)(y)[Rxy \rightarrow Rxx]$. Such inferential connections can be important already in a language even though quantifiers have not yet been introduced to codify them explicitly as the contents of claims. Nontrivial work must be done (and "STSSD" shows that it can be done, and how), to turn the notion of predicate as equivalence class of substitutionally variant sentences, defined here, into the full-blooded notion of a cross-referenced predicate, as will be required for the introduction of quantifiers.

14. It should not be thought that all goodnesses of inference must conform to the preservation model, in that there is a kind of status such that the inference is good if the conclusion has the same status as the premises (any more than it should be thought that all good inferences have some sort of substitutional goodness). The notion of 'transmission' of status is intended to indicate that the possession of a certain status by the premise (for instance, that S is assertionally committed to it) guarantees or provides the reason for the possession of that status by the conclusion. The remarks in the text apply to commitment-preserving inferences (the genus of which deductive inferences are a species), but it should be noted that they need not apply to *entitlement*-preserving inferences (the genus of which inductive inferences are a species). I am grateful to Ernest LePore for pointing this out.

15. The restriction to substitution inferences is required because one may, for instance, infer asymmetrically from the applicability of a singular term to the applicability of a predicate: from "The inventor of bifocals is Benjamin Franklin" to "The inventor of bifocals is an American." These do not count as substitution inferences even in the extended sense allowing replacement of frames, because they cross syntactic categorical boundaries.

16. Sortals, such as 'dog' and 'mammal', might seem to contradict this

claim. For they are distinguished from predicates precisely in having associated with them not only criteria of application but also criteria of identity, and yet they can be materially involved in weakening inferences: "Thera is a dog, so Thera is a mammal." But their criteria of identity apply not to substitutions materially involving the sortals themselves, but to those materially involving the singular terms to which the sortals are applied.

17. What is at issue here is an inferentialist version of the distinction between extensional and nonextensional (or transparent and opaque) occurrences of, typically, singular terms.

18. It need not be denied that occurrences whose significance is not governed in this way are semantically significant in a secondary sense, which can be explained only once the primary sense is understood. This is discussed further along.

19. These examples can only represent the asymmetries at the level of sentences. Singular terms *do not* behave asymmetrically, so real examples of asymmetrically behaving substituted-fors are not forthcoming. Probably the closest one can get in real grammar is sortals. Since they have associated with them criteria of identity for the singular terms they qualify, they are more termlike than predicates. Yet they do have proper inclusions, and a straightforward notion of inferential weakening applies to them, as to predicates. The objection may now occur that these examples show that expressions such as predicates, whose occurrences *do* have asymmetric significances, *can* occur embedded in inferentially inverting contexts, showing that something must be wrong in the analogous argument to the conclusion that substituted-for expressions must have symmetric substitution-inferential significances. This legitimate worry is addressed further along, where the distinction between basic subsentential expressions, which can be substituted for, and derived subsentential expression patterns (frames of derived substitutional category), which can only be replaced (as outermost, hence never embedded), will be invoked.

20. Recall that to take it that *q* is incompatible with *p* is to take it that commitment to *q* precludes entitlement to a commitment to *p*. In this way acknowledgments of material incompatibilities are implicit

in the practices governing adopting attitudes (for instance, undertaking or attributing) toward the same pragmatic statuses of commitment and entitlement that inferences can be distinguished as preserving.

21. Indeed, it could be argued that possession of this reflexive expressive capacity and all that goes with it makes so much difference that it provides a plausible place to draw the line between the linguistic and the nonlinguistic. The line between logical and prelogical languages is in any case important enough that researchers investigating what sorts of languages chimps and dolphins can be taught would be well advised to postpone trying to teach them an extra two hundred terms and predicates and instead try to teach them to use conditionals and quantifiers. But there are important cases where it seems to be worth paying the expressive price for dropping logical sentence-compounding devices. In conversation my colleague Ken Manders suggested the language of projective geometry as an example in this connection. Sometimes 'general points' are appealed to, whose projective properties form a proper subset of the projective properties of other points and so are asymmetrically inferentially related to one another in the way sortals can be: particular points have all the properties of general points but not vice versa. How is this possible? Projective properties are not closed under Boolean operations such as complementation, and one cannot introduce conditional properties—a restriction that has sometimes been seen as puzzling. The present argument explains the unobvious connection between the introduction of general points and the exclusion of negation and the conditional from the language in which projective properties are specified.

22. Notice that this characterization of the conclusion could be accepted even by someone who was not persuaded by the expressive approach to understanding the demarcation of specifically logical vocabulary and so the function of logic.

23. Or the singular terms can be individuated by the transformations. This is the route taken in "STSSD."

24. *Tractatus* 5.62.

5. A Social Route from Reasoning to Representing

1. *Critique of Pure Reason,* A69/B94.
2. Ibid., A68/B93; emphasis added.
3. Ibid., A69/B94.
4. This idea is motivated and explored at greater length in Chapter 1, "Semantic Inferentialism and Logical Expressivism." See also Chapter 2 of Robert B. Brandom, *Making It Explicit* (Cambridge, Mass.: Harvard University Press, 1994).
5. By this criterion, the 'Slab' *Sprachspiel* that Wittgenstein describes early in the *Investigations,* for instance, does not qualify as a genuinely *linguistic* practice. For further discussion of why this is a good way to talk, see my essay "Asserting," *Nous* 17, no. 4 (November 1983): 637–650.
6. There are a myriad technical details that need to be cleared up in order to make an analysis of truth talk along these lines work. I have addressed those difficulties elsewhere: that is where the prosentential or anaphoric account of truth comes in. See Chapter 5 of *Making It Explicit,* and "Pragmatism, Phenomenalism, and Truth Talk," *Midwest Studies in Philosophy* 12 (1988): 75–93, *Realism.* For present purposes, those details can be put to one side.
7. The approach pursued here (including a treatment of both *de dicto* ascriptions and epistemically strong *de re* ascriptions) is presented at length in Chapter 8 of *Making It Explicit.*
8. Obviously, such an account requires emendation to handle the cases where the one to whom a propositional attitude is ascribed would use indexicals, or a different language, to express that attitude. See Chapter 8 of *Making It Explicit.*
9. One way to see that this is right is that the ascription-forming operators can be *iterated:* S' can claim of t that S claims of it that $\phi(\text{it})$. Thus there would in any case be not *two* different kinds of belief (*de dicto* and *de re*) but an infinite number.
10. Daniel Dennett, "Beyond Belief," in *Thought and Object,* ed. A. Woodfield (Oxford: Clarendon Press, 1982), pp. 1–96.
11. This line of thought is worked out in detail in Chapter 4, "What Are Singular Terms, and Why Are There Any?" and in Chapter 6 of *Making It Explicit.*

6. Objectivity and the Normative Fine Structure of Rationality

1. It might be noticed in passing that it is *not* harmless to paraphrase this choice as that between talking about how linguistic expressions *ought* to be used, and how they are *actually* or *in fact* used, or how practitioners are *disposed* to use them. Using an expression correctly or incorrectly is something practitioners can actually or in fact do, something they can be disposed to do. The difference should be located rather in the vocabulary the theorist is permitted to use in characterizing what speakers and audiences actually do and are disposed to do. Formulating this difference as a difference between saying how the language *is* used and how it (only) *ought* to be used is the decisive move in the conjuring trick that lands one in the intractable puzzlements about conceptual normativity that Kripke's Wittgenstein has made familiar.

2. I think of Dretske, Fodor, and Millikan as presenting theories with this general shape. Perhaps Gibbard's very different approach to moral norms, when generalized and adapted to the case of linguistic norms, will find its place here too.

3. My thought is that there is no way to specify the ideality in question that is not either question-begging (in implicitly appealing to a notion of truth) or trivial, in the light of the sensitivity of the practical effects of otherwise more ideal status for one belief both to the *falsity* of collateral beliefs and (even more damaging) to *ignorance* concerning them. I present one argument along these lines in "Unsuccessful Semantics," *Analysis* 54, no. 3 (July 1994): 175–178.

4. It is not identical with inferentialism as introduced in Chapter 1, since that thesis concerned the relative explanatory priority of the concepts of inference and representation, and linguistic rationalism as used here is silent about representation. In *Making It Explicit* (Cambridge, Mass.: Harvard University Press, 1994) [hereafter *MIE*], I distinguish three sorts of inferentialist claims: weak inferentialism, strong inferentialism, and hyperinferentialism. Weak inferentialism is the claim that inferential articulation is a *necessary* aspect of conceptual content. Strong inferentialism is the claim that *broadly* inferential articulation is *sufficient* to determine conceptual content

(including its representational dimension). Hyperinferentialism is the claim that *narrowly* inferential articulation is *sufficient* to determine conceptual content. Broadly inferential articulation includes as inferential the relation even between circumstances and consequences of application, even when one or the other is *non*inferential (as with observable and immediately practical concepts), since in applying any concept one implicitly endorses the propriety of the inference from its circumstances to its consequences of application. Narrowly inferential articulation is restricted to what Sellars calls "language-language" moves, that is, to the relation between propositional contents. Weak inferentialism is the most plausible of these theses. Strong inferentialism is the view endorsed and defended here and in *MIE*. (It is sometimes thought that in his classical inferentialist tract "Inference and Meaning" of 1948, Sellars presents an argument for weak inferentialism but draws strong inferentialist conclusions.) Hyperinferentialism is plausible at most for some abstract mathematical concepts. Linguistic rationalism is a version of weak inferentialism, which the present chapter endeavors to show has some strong inferentialist consequences, when suitably elaborated.

5. It should be remarked that acknowledging incompatibilities means treating the assessment of entitlements as a two-stage process. First, one assesses prima facie claims to entitlement, and then one winnows from this set those commitments that are incompatible with other commitments, and hence precluded from entitlement. What I call (here and in what follows) "entitlement-preserving inferences" structure the inheritance of prima facie commitments.

6. As Crispin Wright has pointed out (in an unpublished comment on this argument), according to the definitions offered here, if two claims differ in their incompatibilities, they can at most be alike in the circumstances in which one is prima facie entitled to them, not in the circumstances in which one is *finally* entitled to them. The assertibilist tradition did not make this distinction, since it did not divide the undifferentiated status of assertibility into commitment and entitlement in the first place (and hence was not in a position to discuss incompatibility). I think a good case can be made for treating the bits

of their motivations that (implicitly) concern entitlement as addressing prima facie entitlements.

7. A fuller telling of this story (such as that in *Making It Explicit*) would distinguish *three* moves beyond classical assertibility theories in order to fund a suitable notion of objective representational content for declarative sentences. The first is the move from treating assertibility as the fundamental normative pragmatic or force-related notion to commitment and entitlement (which then makes it possible to define incompatibility). The second is the move from the *circumstances* under which the normative status in question is acquired (assertibility conditions) to include also *consequences* of acquiring it, as urged in Chapter 1. This is moving toward a notion of content as inferential role, identifying propositional contentfulness as suitability to play the role both of conclusion and of premise in inferences of various sorts. The interaction of this move with the previous one generates the three notions of inference (commitment-preserving, entitlement-preserving, and incompatibility entailments) employed in the text. The third is the move from looking at normative *statuses* (assertibility, commitment, entitlement) to normative *social attitudes*. This is to focus on *attributing* (to others) and *acknowledging* (oneself) commitments and so on as the primary phenomenon. In Chapter 5 I argued that this distinction of *social perspective* is what makes intelligible the specifically *representational* dimension of propositional contents. One might have worried, at the end of that story, about how it is possible (what one has to do in order) to adopt, as it were, a third-person perspective toward one's *own* attitudes, and so take them to be subject in principle to the same sort of assessment to which one subjects the attitudes of others, in offering *de re* specifications of their contents. The argument of this chapter provides the answer to that question.

Index

◆ ◆ ◆